TIME and PLACE

History 1: *Teacher's Book*

Patricia Harrison   Steve Harrison
Paul Davies   Jonathan Hewitt   John Lancaster   Lynn Lancaster
Linda Richardson   Geoff Timmins   Jo Webster

Key Stage 2

SIMON & SCHUSTER
EDUCATION

Text © 1992 Patricia and Steve Harrison, Paul Davies, Jonathan Hewitt, Lynn and John Lancaster, Linda Richardson, Geoff Timmins, Jo Webster, Cathy Wilson
Design and artwork ©
1992 Simon & Schuster Education
Photographs © The sources credited

All rights reserved

First published in 1992 in Great Britain by
Simon & Schuster Education
Campus 400, Maylands Avenue
Hemel Hempstead HP2 7EZ

Printed in Great Britain by
Cambus Litho, East Kilbride

British Library Cataloguing in Publication Data
A catalogue record of this book is available from the British Library

ISBN 0 7501 0311 6

Designed by Vivienne Gordon
Artwork by David Ashby (pages 40, 42, 68, 72, 86, 94, 100, 104)
Richard Deverell (pages 36, 44, 74)
Jackie Gill (pages 64, 96, 99)
Jonathon Heap (chapter logos)
Brian Hoskin (pages 14, 16, 20, 22, 59, 85, 105)
Hussein Hussein (page 32)
Mike Lacey (pages 6, 8, 11, 27, 29, 55, 58)
David McAllister (pages 38, 43, 45)
Chris Orr (pages 46, 53, 90)
Julia Osorno (pages 12, 18, 19, 24, 25, 28, 35, 37, 41, 48, 50, 65, 67, 75, 81, 82)
Pat Thorne (pages 10, 15, 34, 47, 49, 57, 87, 89, 91, 93, 95, 101)
Picture research by Bridget Fleetwood
Typesetting by Janet Goss and Vivienne Gordon

Photocopying
Multiple photocopies of the pages designated A and R in the Contents may be made without payment or the need to seek permission only by the purchasing schools for use in teaching at these schools. In all other cases, permission to photocopy and distribute photocopies of these materials must be sought. The authors and publishers will prosecute any infringement of copyright laws as it affects this work.

Photo credits
Ancient Art & Architecture Collection (pages 11, 21, 28, 29 top centre, 33 middle, 49 bottom left, 55 right, 95 bottom left, 99 bottom) Ashmolean Museum (pages 54, 80 left) Bodleian Library (pages 79 bottom right, 89 bottom right, 98, 106) Bridgeman Art Library (pages 33 right, 34 right) British Library (pages 82, 88, 89 top, 100 bottom, 102) British Museum (pages 23, 24, bottom, 26, 29 centre middle, 34 left, 49 right) Martyn Chillmaid (page 87) Peter Clayton (page 17 top centre) Collections (page 47 left) Mary Evans Picture Library (pages 55 William and Mary, 83 left and right, 101) Werner Forman Archive (page 99 top) Fotomas Index (page 70) Greater London Library (page 119) Guildhall Library, Corporation of London (page 117) Steve Harrison (page 5) Michael Holford (pages 29 bottom left, 53 middle, 55 middle, 91) Hulton Picture Company (pages 80 top right) Kobal Collection (page 17 left and right) Magdalene College Cambridge (page 76 right) Mansell Collection (pages 52, 76 left, 80 bottom right, 82, 83 middle) Ander McIntyre (pages 47 right, 49 top middle, 53, 77 top right, 113, 114, 118) Museum of London (page 77 middle and bottom) National Museums and Galleries on Merseyside (page 33 left) National Portrait Gallery London (pages 55, 63) National Trust (page 79 top right) Rex Features (page 77 bottom) V & A Theatre Museum (page 17 bottom centre)

Cover
Ancient Art & Arcitecture Collection (centre)
Michael Holford (right)

CONTENTS

	Using *Time and Place*	4
	Planning and practice	5
	Information technology	6-7

ANCIENT EGYPT — 8-29

R	Timeline	8
	Ancient Egypt	9
	Archaeology	10
	Looking at artefacts	11
A	Harvest time	12
	Food and farming	13
R	Causes and consequences	14
	The Nile	15
R	People and society	16
R	Cleopatra	17
R	The life of a pharaoh	18
	Religious beliefs	19
R	Embalming	20
R	Life after death	21
R	Gods and goddesses	22
	Science and technology	23
R	Craftworkers	24
	Mathematics	25
	Mummies, medicine and magic	26
	Culture and writing	27
R	Hieroglyphs	28
	Art and architecture	29

INVADERS AND SETTLERS — 30-59

R	Timeline	30
	Romans, Anglo-Saxons and Vikings	31
	The Anglo-Saxons in Britain	32
	The Anglo-Saxons in Britain	33
	The Vikings in Britain	34
R	Reasons for the invasion	35
R	A Celtic settlement	36
	The Roman Conquest	37
R	Into battle	38
	Resistance to Roman rule	39
R	Arms and armour	40
	Way of life of the settlers	41
R	Roman town centre	42
	Town and country	43
R	Silchester: a Roman town	44
	Roman roads	45

R	A Roman villa	46
	Roman buildings	47
R	Map of Roman Britain	48
	Trade and industry	49
A	At work	50
	Religious life	51
R	Evidence in stone	52
	Art and architecture	53
R	Children at play	54
	Entertainment and leisure	55
A	Roman numerals	56
	Legacy	57
R	Romulus and Remus	58
R	The origins of Rome	59

TUDOR AND STUART TIMES — 60-83

R	Timeline	60
	Tudor and Stuart times	61
R	The Tree of Succession	62
	Tudor and Stuart rulers	63
R	A feast fit for a king	64
	Life at court	65
A	A Stuart menu	66
	The break with Rome	67
R	Roundheads and Cavaliers	68
	Civil War and Restoration	69
R	The death warrant of Charles I	70
R	Portraits of the rulers	71
R	Travelling in Tudor and Stuart times	72
	Towns, trade and transport	73
R	Living through the Plague	74
	The Great Plague	75
R	Extracts from Samuel Pepys's Diary	76
	London's burning	77
	Religious changes	78
	James I and religion	79
R	Treason and plot	80
	Exploration and empire	81
R	Views of women	82
	Famous people and their legacies	83

EXPLORATION AND ENCOUNTERS 1450-1550 — 84-107

R	Timeline	84
	Exploration and encounters 1450-1550	85
R	Ship ahoy!	86
	Voyages of exploration: on board ship	87
R	World map 1489	88
	Voyages of exploration: journey into the unknown	89
R	The voyage of Columbus 1492	90
	Voyages of exploration: navigation	91
A	Ship's log	92
	Voyages of exploration: in search of the Spice Islands	93
A	Aztec homelife	94
	Aztec life	95
A	Aztec numbers	96
	Aztec city life	97
R	Aztec education	98
	Aztec culture	99
R	The invasion of Tenochtitlán	100
	The Spanish conquest of the Aztec Empire	101
R	Searching for clues	102
	European and Aztec civilizations: differences	103
R	Crossing the Atlantic	104
	The Spanish Empire: trade	105
R	Slaves in the goldmines	106
	The Spanish Empire: the legacy	107

LOCAL HISTORY — 108-128

R	Education timeline	108
	Local history	109
R	Local History Study Unit: planning sheet	110
	Planning a Local History Study Unit	111
A	Looking at artefacts	112
	Local history sources	113
	Searching for clues	114
	Oral sources	115
	Written sources	116
	Obtaining source material	117
	Schools 100 years ago	118
R	Classroom in 1910	119
	The school curriculum	120
R	School report	121
R	In the playground	122-123
	Teaching and teachers	124
R	Log book extracts	125
	Scholars	126
R	Attendance register	127
	School premises/school plan	128

4 Using Time and Place

Continuity and Progression
Time and Place is a history and geography programme for four to eleven-year-olds. At Key Stage 1, the two subjects are interwoven in themes appropriate to younger children. At Key Stage 2, history and geography are separated.

Organisation of the HSUs
We have divided the HSUs between the lower and upper juniors in a way which we believe is best both for pupils and teachers. Children aged 7-9 have less well developed reading skills than those aged 9-11. It is therefore sensible, with the younger age groups, to concentrate on those HSUs which largely require interpretation of visual evidence. None of the HSUs featured in this book has written material accessible to children without support or translation. The same is not true for Victorian Britain or Britain since 1930, which is why they are in *History 2*.

We believe that a classical civilization should be encountered at both upper and lower junior levels. We have therefore included Ancient Egypt in this book and Ancient Greece in *History 2*. Certain concepts and political ideas developed in Ancient Greece are somewhat abstract and therefore more suited to older children.

The four-year programme for Key Stage 2 is:

Year 3	Year 4	Year 5	Year 6
Invaders and Settlers	Tudor and Stuart Times	Victorian Britain	Britain since 1930
Ancient Egypt	Explorations and Encounters	Ancient Greece	Writing and printing

Local history support is given in both books. One local history study unit must be taught at Key Stage 2.

If class sizes allow, this arrangement facilitates a chronological approach to the British HSUs. However, Years 3/4 are combined in *History 1* and Years 5/6 in *History 2* so that the teachers who have mixed-age classes can teach a two-year rolling programme.

Teacher Knowledge
A key component of each section is background information for the teacher. The National Curriculum in history has a large knowledge base and many generalist primary class teachers have felt under-equipped to cope with the volume and depth of content. *Time and Place* aims to give teachers the confidence to handle the content of the period being studied and the sources.

Background Information
The Tudor and Stuart period began just over 500 years ago at the end of the Middle Ages, when Henry Tudor, a member of the Welsh branch of the Tudor family, was crowned. He was the first Tudor monarch. The period ended at the beginning of the

How do we Know?
Our approach throughout is not to give children the answers but to encourage them to look for clues, investigate and interrogate evidence, search for corroborative evidence and constantly raise the question: How do we know?

We have used an approach on the Resource Sheets which gives the children very little textual instruction. The Teacher's Notes at the foot of each sheet (which we suggest are masked before photocopying) demonstrate the flexibility of this resource and that the tasks are designed to match different Statements of Attainment at different levels. This means that a mixed-ability group or class can use the same resource.

Teacher Resources
The Activity Sheets are indicated in the Contents by A. They may be photocopied and are intended to be completed by the children.

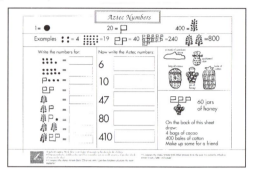

The Resources Sheets, indicated in the Contents by R, are designed to provide the teacher with a range of classroom resources which will stimulate and motivate the children. These include portraits, photographs of artefacts, games, artists' reconstructions of past events and buildings.

We suggest that teachers enlarge these on a photocopier, mount them on card and laminate them for longer life. The increasing availability of colour photocopiers, both in teachers' centres and in commercial bureaux, means that many of the full-colour resources in this book can be copied and used with children.

PLANNING AND PRACTICE 5

ASSESSMENT AND RECORDING

Assessment should be an integral part of planning and practice. The tasks suggested in the Activity and Resource Sheets can also be used for assessment purposes. The teacher will need to select the task she/he decides to use for that purpose and collect evidence in terms of the child's responses. The results should be recorded. For example, on a number of occasions, the children will meet tasks which ask them to distinguish between 'fact' and 'point of view'. (AT 2, Level 3). Sometimes we suggest the teacher writes a range of statements which match the categories and asks the children to sort them. At other times, we suggest the children might write statements for other children to categorise. This is obviously a more advanced task and will only be possible after substantial experience of the former activity. Teachers should decide which of the proposed tasks will be used for assessment and use them accordingly.

A planning grid is provided on the introductory page of each section in the book. It indicates which Statements of Attainment can be addressed through activities provided in that section. This is designed to aid teachers in their planning and recording.

EXAMPLES OF TASKS/QUESTIONS ACROSS LEVELS OF ATTAINMENT

The Teacher's Notes accompanying the Local Studies section demonstrate how each source relates to Statements of Attainments across Levels 2 to 4. We offer this support to demonstrate the potential of the resources and increase teacher confidence when using them. We would suggest that all children have the opportunity of experiencing activities across Levels and are not restricted within one Level.

USING THE TIMELINES

There is a timeline at the beginning of each section in this book. It can be used in a number of ways:
- It can be enlarged and cut into sections to make one continuous timeline along a wall
- Individual 'events' can be cut out. The children can work in groups to research each and place them in chronological order.
- Sections from a timeline can be used to support the Statements of Attainment. For example, three events could be chosen and the children asked to find out why the people acted as they did. (AT 1, Level 2b)
- The children could use two or more timelines together to compare and contrast features, look for similarites and differences. (AT 1, Level 3c) For example, compare Tenochtitlán with a Roman town.
- Look for things which changed or stayed the same. (AT 1, Level 4) For example, legacy of the Romans in Britain or looking at Egypt over 3000 years.
- In this way, the children would be putting together information drawn from a range of historical sources (AT 3, Level 4) including the full-colour two-metre timeline, photographs and 'How do we know?' posters in the Resource Pack.
- Teachers can devise 'fact' and 'point of view' statements for each timeline. For example, Henry VIII had six wives. [Fact] Henry VIII was a cruel, selfish king. [Point of view]
- A timeline can be used alongside maps. The children could trace developments over time and add them, either pictorially or in written form, to the appropriate map with dates.

PRIMARY AND SECONDARY SOURCES

The children should have access to a range of sources. Primary sources are contemporaneous sources: for example, photographs, artefacts, written documents, newspapers, portraits, carvings (or photographs of). Secondary sources include artists' impressions. These are useful when dealing with reconstructions, as most adults and children have difficulty in mentally reconstructing, for example, a building from its foundation stones. It is important that teachers ensure that artists' reconstructions are based on evidence and not a figment of their imagination. For example, amphitheatres in Britain were made from wood and earth, not stone.

ANACHRONISTIC PHOTOGRAPHS

Photographic reconstructions, such as a Roman soldier, are useful sources but children should realise that they *are reconstructions*. Encourage the children to investigate them. The following true exchange is illuminating:

Teacher: 'Is he a real Roman?'
Child: 'Yes.'
Teacher: 'Whom do you think took the photograph?'
Child: 'The captain.'
Teacher: 'What kind of camera do you think he used?'
Child: 'Oh, a *very* old one. It was a long time ago, one of those where a black cloth goes over your head.'

The teacher went on to encourage the children to look for other evidence to test their views.

6 INFORMATION TECHNOLOGY

In *History: Non-statutory Guidance*, it is recognised that:
• IT can help with historical enquiry and in communicating the results of historical study.
• History can contribute to the ATs in technology.
Specifically:
• Word-processing and desk-top publishing (DTP) programs offer excellent means for children to display and present their findings.
• Database programs are ideal for recording findings as children examine source material (AT 3) then investigate their results (AT 1).
• Simulations are an exciting way for children to explore historical situations, discover facts, investigate different interpretations or ask questions (AT 2).
• Overlay keyboards or art programs can be used effectively for maps, pictures, labelling etc.

It is important to stress to the children that simulated newspaper, radio or video accounts of the past are our way of viewing the past. Remind the children that people in the past did not have newspapers, radio or TV.

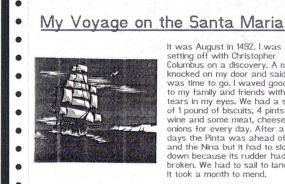

PRESENTING INFORMATION

My Voyage on the Santa Maria

It was August in 1492. I was setting off with Christopher Columbus on a discovery. A man knocked on my door and said it was time to go. I waved goodbye to my family and friends with tears in my eyes. We had a supply of 1 pound of biscuits, 4 pints of wine and some meat, cheese and onions for every day. After a few days the Pinta was ahead of us and the Nina but it had to slow down because its rudder had broken. We had to sail to land and it took a month to mend.

There are a variety of word-processing and DTP programs available for Years 3 and 4. (Some word processing programs, such as Whow, allow the teacher to set up a word bank for children to use.) With these programs, children can:
• Draft and redraft their own stories about life on one of Drake's voyages, a Viking invasion, the life of a Roman soldier or other stories where the child takes part in the historical situation.
• Write diaries of historical events, or the life of a famous person: for example, life during the Plague or a diary of Boudicca.
• Make newspapers covering past events, such as the Fire of London, with 'eye witness' accounts.
• Write their descriptions of historical change, or present their findings of a historical study.
• Produce their own labels for artefacts, displays, maps and pictures using the large fonts available with many programs.

HANDLING INFORMATION

Database programs can be used to investigate historical sources. Children making their own files and entering information are useful ways of keeping a record of their findings as they examine source material: artefacts, newspapers and photographs, for instance. They can take a typical day in their life, pick out and describe the objects or 'artefacts' which they use, then do a similar study for a person living in another period, say Tudor England.

This information can be entered in such fields as those shown here.

Name: Peter S
Artefact: glass bottle
Time: about 100 years ago
Use: beer or pop
Materials: glass
Where obtained: dug from waste ground next to an old factory
Description: made of thick glass, a sort of green colour. It has a marble in the top instead of a bottle top

ASKING QUESTIONS

Such information entered into a database can be searched by the children to look for comparisons. For example:

How many items have you used today that were not used in Tudor times?

Which items can you find in Tudor times and today but which are made from different materials?

How many items were made at home in Tudor times? How many items have you used today which were made at home?

Romans, Anglo-Saxons and Vikings

Background Information

The problem most teachers face with the Invaders and Settlers HSU is what to exclude. The individual themes of Romans, Anglo-Saxons and Vikings could each fill a term. So, the first task in planning this HSU is to decide on the depth and balance of work the children will meet.

The Invaders and Settlers HSU *does not require* a detailed treatment of *all three* components. The requirement is to provide the children with an *overview* of the 1000-year period and a *deeper study of any one* of the three components. This book focuses on the Roman conquest, with background information provided on the Anglo-Saxon and Viking periods.

The overview of the whole period should highlight similarities and differences within the themes of Invasion and Settlement.

Migration

The period from the later Roman Age to the end of the first millennium was marked by large-scale movements of population in Europe. Some were communities moving in search of land to farm and to settle. Among the similarities with today that children might identify are:
- Economic motives – people in search of opportunities for a better standard of living.
- Conflict motives – people escaping from warfare.

Invaders or Settlers?

The distinction between the Roman incursion into Britain and those of the Anglo-Saxons and Vikings need to be clearly delineated. The Roman invasion and settlement were motivated by military and economic considerations (particularly the mineral resources). They did not involve a mass movement of population, and the settlement was essentially urban. The Anglo-Saxon invasions were not coordinated or strategically planned. The attacks were made, over a period of some 400 years, by several distinct groups, each of whose intention was to settle and farm the land they conquered. The cumulative effect was the movement of large numbers of people – both into and out of Britain. The Vikings invasion, too, had a similar military phase followed by large-scale settlement.

The Past in the Present

An enquiry-based approach to the total theme involves searching for evidence today which points to the invasions and settlements of the past.

Provide the children with OS maps from various parts of Britain. Include the west country, the Brighton area (South Downs), Lincoln, the Humber Estuary, Middlesbrough and the North Yorkshire Moors, Manchester, Chester, the Llyn Peninsula and the Lake District. (A cheaper way is to dismantle a large-scale motoring atlas and use the individual pages.)

The various maps should be analysed by the children working in groups. Using place-name evidence, they should focus their enquiry on the following questions:
- Is there a single settler group shown here?
- If there is more than one group, is there a pattern to where they are?
- Is there a physical feature (mountain, river …) separating one group from another?

Origins of Place-Names

A blank map of the British Isles can be used to collate the results of the children's enquiries. What emerges is a Celtic (British) western extremity, a Saxon central band running the length of England, mixed Saxon/Viking areas in the east and north-west of England, and a few, widely scattered Roman settlements.

The Invaders and Settlers HSU can therefore begin as an investigation into these four peoples who have left their mark on modern Britain: Who were they?

Where did they come from? When did they arrive?

	HISTORY											
ATTAINMENT TARGETS	**1**								**2**		**3**	
LEVELS	2			3			4			2	3 4	2 3	4
STATEMENTS	a	b	c	a	b	c	a	b	c	a	a a	a a	a
30 Timeline	•	•	•	•	•	•	•	•					
31 Romans, Anglo-Saxons, Vikings	•	•	•	•	•	•	•	•					
32-33 The Anglo-Saxons											• •	•	•
34 The Vikings											• •	•	•
35 Reasons for invasion		•		•	•		•	•				•	
36 A Celtic settlement		•		•			•					•	
37 The Roman conquest	•	•		•	•		•	•				•	
38 Into battle	•	•	•	•			•						
39 Resistance to Roman rule		•		•			•	•				•	
40 Arms and armour		•		•			•					•	•
41 Way of life of the settlers	•			•			•					•	•
42 Roman town centre	•	•	•	•			•					•	•
43 Town and country	•	•		•			•					•	•
44 Silchester: A Roman town		•		•			•					•	•
45 Roman roads	•	•		•	•		•					•	•
46 A Roman villa		•		•			•					•	•
47 Roman buildings		•	•	•			•					•	•
48 Map of Roman Britain				•	•		•					•	
49 Trade and industry	•			•			•					•	•
50 At work		•		•			•						
51 Religious life		•		•	•		•					•	•
52 Evidence in stone	•	•		•			•					• •	•
53 Art and architecture	•			•			•					•	•
54 Children at play		•					•					• •	
55 Entertainment and leisure		•		•	•		•					•	•
56 Roman numerals		•		•	•		•					•	
57 Legacy		•	•	•	•		•					•	
58 Romulus and Remus	•			•		•	•		•				
59 The origins of Rome													

Anglo-Saxon	**Viking**	**British/Celtic**
field, feld = field	by = village	pen = hill, headland
ford = river crossing	erg, arch = pasture	tre = farm
ham = village	fell = mountain	**Roman**
ing = tribe	holme = island	Apart from the
ley, leigh = clearing	ness = land near water	'*chester, caster, cester*' variants,
ton = village	thorpe = village	Roman place-names
wick, wich = farm	thwaite = clearing (often near water)	need to be noted individually.

32 The Anglo-Saxons in Britain

Background Information

The withdrawal of the Roman army from Britain was completed by AD 407. It was not a sudden abandonment. As more soldiers were needed by Rome to fight the Huns, Roman legions had been gradually withdrawn from Britain during the latter part of the occupation, yet evidence would suggest that some residual Roman administration continued beyond 407. But without the Romans, the native Britons were helpless against the waves of invaders who had started to arrive.

The invasions of what had been Roman Britain were not solely from the south and east by Anglo-Saxons. Scots and Irish groups raided and settled western Britain. The Picts were active in northern Scotland and on the east coast of England. It was a time of upheaval and population movement. Large numbers of native Britons left southern and south-western England for what is now called Brittany.

The helpless Britons recruited Saxon mercenaries to defend their settlements. These mercenaries had already served in the Roman army in Britain. They had a reputation as fine soldiers. In the early 440s, rebellious groups of these mercenaries decided to settle their own land in Britain, mainly Kent and Sussex. Their influence and control gradually spread, but were temporarily checked in about AD 500 after a pitched battle with the native Britons.

ANGLO-SAXON KINGDOMS
Towards the end of the 6th century, several Anglo-Saxon kingdoms had been established. Kent, Sussex, Essex, Wessex, East Anglia, Mercia, Northumbria and Dumnonia were the more powerful ones, but borders were fluid and smaller kingdoms existed as did relatively independent areas within the larger kingdoms.

In the 7th century, Northumbria was the most powerful kingdom. But Mercia's power and influence were growing and it became the dominant kingdom of the 8th century, effectively exercising hegemony over most of the southern kingdoms. Wessex challenged Mercia's supremacy in the 9th century and was to remain the sole 'English' kingdom, as Northumbria, Mercia and East Anglia were subsequently conquered by Vikings.

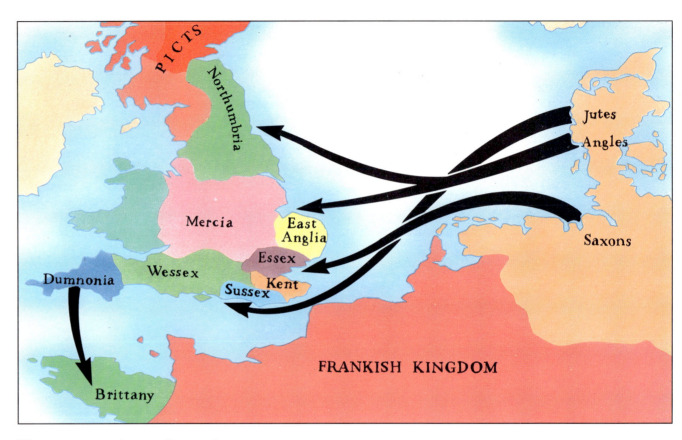

Who were the Anglo-Saxons?

The term 'Anglo-Saxon' covers various distinct groups who settled in Britain between the 5th and 8th centuries: the Angles (from southern Denmark), the Jutes (from northern Denmark and northern Germany), the Saxons (from north-western Germany – Saxony) and the Frisians (from northern Netherlands – Friesland). Other settlers came from the Frankish kingdoms (northern France).

The Angles settled in north and eastern England, which became, respectively, Angles-land (England) and East Anglia. The Jutes and Frisians occupied south-eastern England. The Saxons settled across southern England. Today, the county names of Essex (East Saxon) and Sussex (South Saxon) commemorate their presence. The kingdom of Wessex (west Saxon) has long since vanished.

Independent areas
The Anglo-Saxons ended their westward expansion at Offa's Dyke. Wales remained unconquered (parts of it still remain unanglicised). The south-western kingdom of Dumnonia was the last part of modern England to integrate with Angles-land. Place names in Cornwall still provide evidence of a richly independent development.

The Anglo-Saxons in Britain

The Dark Ages
Anglo-Saxon England covers part of the period traditionally known as the Dark Ages. The name reflects the dearth of information about the period compared with the Roman occupation and the Norman era. Unfortunately, the term Dark Ages has had connotations of grimness and despair even of chaos and anarchy. Such an impression is seriously misleading. The Anglo-Saxon colonisation produced a flourishing culture, of which the greatest legacy is the English language.

The children could compare the designs of Anglo-Saxon jewellery with those of the Romans.

Settlements
There is relatively little Anglo-Saxon building which has survived. The Anglo-Saxons were not attracted to the urban society which still existed in Britain after the Roman withdrawal (particularly in southern England). They were farmers, unaccustomed to town life. Their settlement pattern was to establish farmsteads and small villages but not large towns. This general picture was slightly different in the Kent area, where some of the settlers were Franks with a tradition of town dwelling.

There is a long-held view that the Anglo-Saxons destroyed urban centres but the evidence is unconvincing. It is more likely that towns decayed as a consequence of neglect and the fading of an administrative infrastructure which could support urban life and industry.

The Anglo-Saxons lived in wooden houses, hence the lack of archaeological evidence. This has produced an over-reliance on burial sites as a source of evidence for the Anglo-Saxon culture. What such evidence does reveal, however, is a continuity of cultural practices in parallel with those in the Anglo-Saxon homelands.

Virtually nothing is known about the farming methods of the early Anglo-Saxon settlers. Most extant manuscripts which refer to farming are from the 900s onwards and it would be misleading to extrapolate such evidence to earlier dates.

Alfred the Great
By AD 878 Danish invaders had conquered most of eastern Mercia, East Anglia and Northumbria, and were threatening Wessex – ruled by Alfred since 871. The Danes demanded payment to remain outside Wessex and Alfred succumbed. But the Danes, led by Guthrum, welshed on the deal and in 878 attacked Wessex, defeating Alfred's army. Alfred hid in the Athelney Fens, while many of his supporters fled abroad.

Alfred soon gathered another army and defeated the Danes. Under the Treaty of Chippenham, Guthrum agreed to leave Wessex and to become a Christian. Alfred took London in 886, and in the same year had a pact with Guthrum which effectively divided England into two spheres of influence demarcated by the old Roman Watling Street. The Danish area was called Danelaw. The English in Danelaw and the Danes in the English area were each guaranteed their own rights and customs.

Achievements
Through Alfred's reorganisation of the English armies, the landowning thanes became a better organised, equipped and trained military class. Under his 'laws', which placed a high priority on loyalty to authority, society was divided into three classes: those who prayed, those who fought and those who worked. The fyrd was reorganised so that a standing army was always available, even during planting and harvesting. Burghs, fortified strongholds, were established which provided a defence at vulnerable points. Alfred also re-established the importance of a navy. In practice, his navy was not effective. The newly-designed ships were crewed by Frisians, who had difficulty sailing them.

Among his other achievements was Alfred's support for learning. Latin was revived, translations into Anglo-Saxon were begun and the Anglo-Saxon chronicles established.

Christianity
The Christianity of Celtic Britain had become increasingly independent of Rome, and was based essentially on the monasteries. Irish monks travelled far and wide as missionaries. St Columba (cAD 521-597) established a centre at Iona from which missions were sent to the Picts and to the Angles of northern England. One such, under Aidan, introduced Celtic Christianity to Northumbria. It led to the founding of monasteries in northern England, such as Lindisfarne, which became great centres of learning.

Simultaneously, Pope Gregory the Great's policy of establishing Papal authority throughout Europe was bearing fruit. St Augustine and a band of 40 monks arrived at Thanet in AD 597 and began a successful campaign of conversion to Roman Christianity.

The Celtic and Roman Christian movements were mutually suspicious of each other. They united in about AD 664, with the Roman tradition ultimately being nationally adopted.

The children could compare and contrast how Romans, Saxons and Vikings depicted their religious beliefs.

The Vikings in Britain

Britain as Part of a Wider Viking World
The Viking invasions of England should be seen in the context of a wider Viking expansion.

The term 'Viking' embraces the Scandinavian people of Denmark, Norway and Sweden who travelled in every direction in a remarkable period of expansion and exploration, from the late 8th century until the 11th century.

According to the popular image of the Vikings, they were murdering, raping plunderers – uncivilised people who destroyed churches and societies. Most of our sources for the Viking's history in England are the biased chronicles of the monks who suffered the Viking incursions, and so a broader interpretation of the Vikings' activities should be pursued.

Many Vikings settled in Ireland and established its main towns, including Dublin. In eastern and northwestern England, they became established as farmers and intermarried with the Saxon population. They colonised the lands of the far north – Faroes, Iceland, Greenland and possibly North America. They became the ruling class in Russia (Rus was the name given to Scandinavians in the east), provided the Imperial guard at Byzantium, and established dynasties in Normandy which went on to conquer England and Sicily.

Vikings buried their possessions before a battle. The Cuerdale hoard, buried in AD 905, is the largest of all known Viking hoards.

'Viking' was originally the West Norse word for someone who fights at sea. And it was from the sea that they launched their first recorded raid on western Europe, at Lindisfarne, in AD 793. Contemporaneous chronicles had difficulty in distinguishing Norwegian, Danish and Swedish Vikings. Their languages, dress, arts and some customs were similar, although certain regional differences in worship and laws existed. They were usually referred to as 'Northmen' or 'Danes' or 'Heathens'.

In AD 835, the Viking attacks intensified. Initially, coastal raids occurred from bases in Ireland, the continental mainland and Scandinavia itself. In 850 they wintered in Thanet. Gradually, their expeditions moved inland. In 865, the first payment of Danegeld took place – peace bought in return for money. Also in 856, a force of more than 2000 Danes invaded Northumbria and in 866 captured York. In turn, the English kingdoms either were defeated or made terms. This army moved around England for more than 15 years. Most of them eventually settled in England.

During the 10th century, Viking rule was gradually overthrown by the kings of Wessex, and England became a single kingdom. Within the Danelaw, however, the settlers were allowed to maintain their own laws and customs. The extent of Scandinavian place-name evidence and the number of Scandinavian names adopted into the English language indicate continued immigration following major invasions. Most of eastern England was settled by Danes, whereas northwestern England was settled by a mixture of Danes and Norwegians, many of whom came via Ireland, Scotland and the Isle of Man. The Vikings later renewed their attacks on England. In AD 991, a fleet of 93 Viking ship arrived in southern England, and from then until 1016 Viking armies invaded frequently. The price of peace (Danegeld) went up each year as the invaders were paid *not* to attack:

for example, 16 000 lbs of silver in 994; 24 000 lbs in 1002.

In 1002, King Aethelred ordered all Danes in England to be killed. Danish reprisals followed in 1003. In 1006, Danegeld reached 36 000 lbs of silver. By 1012 it was 48 000 lbs.

In 1013, Svein Forkbeard and his son Cnut launched a full-scale invasion. They landed at Sandwich, Kent, and conquered the whole of England within months. Svein died during the campaign and Cnut was forced to return to Denmark.

Cnut returned in 1015. In 1016 he won the Battle of Ashingdon and became king of all England. England became a key component of Cnut's northern empire, which included Scotland, Denmark, Norway and part of Sweden.

Cnut died in 1035, whereupon his empire broke up. In 1066, King Harold Hardrada of Norway invaded England in an attempt to re-create a northern empire but was defeated by Harold Godwinson. The Viking age in England was closed but the new conqueror from Normandy, the future William I, had his own Viking connections: his great-great-great-grandfather was Rollo – a Viking chief given land at the mouth of Seine on condition that he stopped other Vikings sailing along it.

Teacher's notes. *Mask these notes before photocopying this sheet for the children.*
This map of the Roman Empire sheet can be used in a number of ways:
• Mask the outer frame and enlarge the map on a photocopier.
• Copy the map onto an OHP transparency, project on to paper to make a large wall map. The children's writing, and artwork can then be displayed around the map. (see Trade and Industry page 49)

• The 'Reasons for Invasion' could be enlarged, copied onto card and laminated. In pairs, the children could sort into 'Probable Reasons' and 'Improbable Reasons'. On each occasion they would have to say why they so concluded.
• The children can cross the improbable reasons and tick the probable. Sort the probable in order of importance.
• Ask them to compare Roman, Saxon and Viking motives for invasions.

Celtic Settlement

Teacher's notes. *Mask these notes before photocopying this sheet for the children.*
- The children could describe what is taking place. Particular attention should be placed on the materials and tools being used (technology), the activities, and the roles of men and women. Compare with the homes and lives of people in Saxon and Viking times and today. Personal research should extend this.
- What evidence is there for the main economic activities of the Britons? Ask the children to classify the range of animal and food products and what each might have been used for.
- They can sequence the steps involved in building a Celtic home. Classroom models should be made using appropriate materials.
- Make comparisons with Roman villas to explore similarities and differences. The teacher needs to emphasise that while some Britons were Romanised and adopted Roman ways, the vast majority were not.

THE ROMAN CONQUEST

BACKGROUND INFORMATION

Considerable trade and communication existed between Britain and mainland Europe before the Roman invasion. The Celtic tribes exported grain, cattle, gold, silver, iron, hides, slaves and hunting dogs, and in return bought ivory, wine, glass and pottery.

As the Roman armies advanced westwards, many Gauls took refuge in Britain. Celtic support of the Gauls antagonised the Romans. This led to an attack by Julius Caesar in 55 BC and again in 54 BC. However, no conquest was undertaken.

Interest in Britain was renewed under the Emperor Claudius. His need for a military victory, plus the Roman belief in their right to rule anywhere, prompted an attempt to conquer Britain. Claudius may also have been attracted by the resources Britain had to offer, while at the same time eliminating its use as a safe haven for rebels.

In AD 43, the Emperor Claudius sent four legions to conquer Britain. Some tribes welcomed the Romans, while others resisted but were defeated, one by one. Aulus Plautius commanded the army, but Claudius probably came over briefly. Between AD 43 and 47 south-east Britain was conquered. Further conquests came between AD 78 and 84, led by the governor Gnaeus Agricola. As a result, only Scotland remained undefeated.

WHAT IS AN INVASION?

Ask the children what they think an invasion is. They should consider what would happen if an aggressor invaded their locality. How would they feel? What would they do personally? What would they expect adults to do? Where would they hope help might come from?

INVASIONS PAST AND PRESENT

It is useful for children to recognise that 'invasion' occurs throughout history and is not confined to the distant past. Many countries in the world have been subject to invasions this century.

The children can carry out personal research and a data-collection exercise based on invasions within living memory. They should interview parents, grandparents, friends and visitors to school.

The questions to be asked can be generated through discussion and presented on a data-collection sheet produced on a word processor. An example is shown here.

```
Conflict between _____ Year _____

Invaders _____ Invaded _____

Reasons


Persons interviewed _____

I remember


I felt
```

RESPONSES

Because this survey will be carried out among people living in Britain in the 1990s, specific invasions will figure prominently. For example:

World War I
World War II
Suez
Vietnam
Falklands
Gulf War

Some children may consider whether such a survey carried out in other parts of the world would produce similar results.

ANALYSING THE DATA

The children should look for patterns in the reponses.

- Does invasion always result in armed conflict?
- Does the initial aggressor usually succeed?
- Do the reasons given by respondents differ? [Interpretations of history]
- What similarities can be seen between 20th century invasions and the Roman invasion?

IMAGINATIVE WRITING

It is worthwhile asking the children to write about an imaginary or actual invasion. The purpose of the activity is to provide the teacher with insights into children's grasp of why invasions take place and how those invaded respond. Such responses may include armed struggle, passive resistance, refugee status or even an open-armed welcome. The children should be encouraged to produce realistic accounts. Any writing should be free of extra-terrestrials and should not end with 'and then I woke up'.

Into Battle

Teacher's notes. *Mask these notes before photocopying this sheet for the children.*
- Describe what you can see and identify differences and similarities between the armies.
- Some children could research the superiority of the Roman army in more depth.
- The children could make models and report to their peers on the role and function of the weapons used.
- The children could do an 'on-the-spot' commentary on a battle between Romans and Celts and draw inferences about who was likely to win. Use a tape recorder and include sound effects, but remind the children that no such reporting was possible then.

Resistance to Roman Rule

Background Information

The Roman army was highly trained and well equipped. Each soldier was thoroughly drilled in fighting techniques and battle formations.

The army was divided into legions, each of which had ten cohorts. A cohort comprised six centuries: each century had one hundred men and was commanded by a centurion.

Compared with the disciplined Romans, the British warriors appeared un-coordinated. This superiority was accentuated by the Romans' various large war machines, such as the catapult (which fired arrows) and the ballista (a giant catapult which hurled huge stones). The Roman army also had low 'sheds' and high towers on wheels with which to approach enemy walls. Under the protection of the shed, they could ram walls or dig underneath them to weaken their foundations. With the tower, they could scale battlements.

One of the most famous Roman fortifications is Hadrian's Wall, which was started in AD 120 and took nine years to build. The Emperor Hadrian built it to protect Roman Britain from raids by the Picts and the Scots. It stretched from Bowness on the Solway Firth to Wallsend on the River Tyne (just over 100 km). It was 4-5 m high and 2-5 m wide. There was a fort every mile, and between the forts were two turrets. On the north side of the wall there was a deep fighting ditch. On the south side, there was another ditch, or vallum, edged by mounds.

The Romans ruled Britain for over 350 years. However, from AD 250 onwards, Roman strongholds were put under increased pressure. Despite Hadrian's Wall, the Picts carried out raids, as did the Scots. The greatest pressure came from the Angles and Saxons, who had begun to raid the south-east of Britain – a region which had previously been exempt from attack. In response, the Romans built a series of forts around the coast: for example, at Dubris (Dover) and Gariannonum (Burgh Castle). The Romans were unable to maintain sufficient defences in Britain due to the military threats to Rome itself. Roman power was further weakened as a result of internal divisions over who should rule the empire.

From AD 300, soldiers were withdrawn to protect Rome from the 'Barbarians'. By AD 410, all legions had left, and British appeals to the Emperor Honorius for help against the invading Saxons were rejected.

Tell the Story of Caratacus

Caratacus and his brother Togodumnus were leaders of the Trinovantes, a British tribe based near St Albans. When the Roman general Plautius and his army invaded Britain in AD 43, the brothers each raised his own army and raced separately to fight the invaders. Both their armies were defeated, so they decided to join forces at Rochester, on the River Medway. They destroyed the bridge at Rochester and were confident they were safe.

'They can't reach us now,' thought Caratacus, but he was wrong. The Roman soldiers were trained to cross the strongest rivers, fully armed. They took the Britons by surprise and killed their horses so they could no longer use their chariots. The battle raged for two days and many men were killed on both sides. Togodumnus was killed and the Britons wanted revenge. Caratacus appealed to the Welsh tribes: 'Join me and fight the Romans.'

With his new army, Caratacus was ready to fight the Romans once again. In Rome, the emperor Claudius called upon General Ostorius to take the place of Plautius. 'Go to Britain and rid us of that nuisance Caratacus.'

The two armies met near the River Severn. Once more Caratacus thought he would win. 'Even if they get up this hill, they'll never get into the fort.' But Caratacus had again underestimated the strength of the well-trained Roman army. In their 'turtle' formation, they climbed the hill and overran the fort. Caratacus fled to Brigantia, in northern England, but his wife and children were taken prisoners.

Caratacus pleaded with Queen Cartimandua of Brigantia to help him fight the Romans, but the Queen was friendly with them. 'The Romans will reward me well if I hand him over,' she thought, and secretly summoned General Ostorius. The Queen gave Caratacus to the General, who sent him to Rome, where he was paraded before the Emperor Claudius.

'Caratacus has shown great courage. Because we Romans admire courageous men, I, Claudius, will spare his life.' So Caratacus spent the rest of his life as a prisoner in Rome.

> **Using the Story**
> The children can retell the story using captions. Discuss why some Celts, such as Caratacus and Boudicca, resisted Roman rule. Consider Queen Cartimandua's motives and Claudius's reactions.

Boudicca

Cassius described Boudicca 100 years after her death.

She was very tall and looked terrifying with a fierce glint in her eyes and a harsh voice. A great mass of red hair hung down to her hips.

Here is another translation of Cassius's description.

She was huge and frightening to look at, with a mass of ginger hair that hung down to her hips. Her voice was as harsh as her looks. She dressed in a multi-coloured tunic with a thick cloak, fastened by a brooch, flung over it. She wore a heavy gold necklace. She shook a spear to terrify all who watched her.

Divide the class into two groups. Give each group one of the descriptions from which they should produce an illustration. They can compare and discuss differences to highlight the problems of finding out about the past. The teacher can draw attention to: the issue of 'translation', the time of writing, the descriptions used and the potential bias of the author.

Can the children identify agreed facts, such as her leading the Iceni in revolt? Or such points of view as her 'harsh' voice?

Arms and Armour

Extract from Tacitus (written in AD 58)

The Attack on Maiden Castle

"The struggle... was fierce. As long as the Britons could hurl spears, rocks and arrows they could win. The Romans advanced under a tortoise shell formation of shields, and broke through the enemy's wall. Hand-to-hand fighting followed. The Britons fled up the hill. The Romans eagerly followed. Both auxiliaries and legionaries forced their way to the summit under a hail of spears. The Britons without breast plates and helmets could not hold out."

Look at the evidence

Make a list of the reasons why you think the Romans won

 Teacher's notes. *Mask these notes before photocopying this sheet for the children.*
This sheet can be used in a number of ways:
- Discuss with the children the nature of the evidence, visual and written, and how this helps us to answer questions about the past.
- Working alone or in pairs, the children could identify evidence pointing to reasons why the Romans defeated the Celts militarily. Differences in equipment could be circled.
- Discuss Tacitus as a source. Was he a Roman or a Celt? Can we separate fact from opinion in his account? When was he writing? Would he have been there?
- The children could carry out personal research into the names of clothes and equipment of warriors on both sides. The illustrations could then be labelled.

Way of Life of the Settlers 41

Background Information

Many veteran soldiers and former Celt chieftains were rewarded with land and houses in the towns and country. They held positions of civic importance in the law courts and council chambers. Below these in importance were skilled workers, such as architects. Poorer citizens (mainly Celts) worked as artisans – carpenters, potters, brick and tile makers, stone cutters and shopkeepers.

For many Celts, life did not change significantly under Roman rule. They remained as farmers, living in their traditional huts, perhaps selling produce in the local town market. This was particularly true for Celts in the north and west of Britain.

Slaves were workers with no rights or status, who were owned by wealthy Romans and Celts. They were either manual labourers, who were working in building, mining or farming, or domestic servants.

The Romans brought with them new fashions. Men wore short-sleeved tunics, over which cloaks could be wrapped in colder weather. Important men wore a toga on special occasions. Tunics were also worn by women, but often augmented by a dress (called a stolla). A wrap (palla) was sometimes draped over the dress. Children dressed like their parents.

Clothes were usually made from wool but wealthy people sometimes wore garments made from linen, cotton or silk. Poorer people were restricted to natural coloured clothes, but wealthier people had a choice of colours, made from vegetable, animal and mineral dyes. Leather slippers, sandals or boots were common footwear. Clothes were fastened with pins, brooches and buttons. Wealthier women were adorned with rings, necklaces, earrings and bracelets.

Women's hair was ornately styled by slaves into combinations of plaits and curls. Men wore short hair and were clean shaven.

Chalk, ashes and coloured earth were all used in the making of cosmetics. Chalk whitened skin, rouge was applied to cheeks and lips, and eyebrows were blackened.

In towns, wealthy people lived in large, detached houses made from stone, built around a courtyard. Some had a second storey. Poorer people lived in tenements, which consisted of long, narrow blocks of rooms, often made from wood.

Fashion
The children could make two-dimensional models to illustrate Roman fashions.

Home Interiors
Collect information on features of Roman homes and compare them with today's.

Clothing for Men
The children could make and wear Roman costume.

Food

A Rich Person's Menu

First course
Baked stuffed dormouse
Snails
Oysters

Mulsum (honey and wine)

Second course
Roast beef and pheasant
Boiled ham
(all served with spicy fish sauce)
Hot bread rolls

Italian wine

Third course
Choose from
Dried and fresh fruit
Stuffed dates fried in honey
Pastries

A Poor Person's Menu
Bread
Vegetable stew
Beer

Asking Questions

Which of these foods do you eat?

Which foods were produced in Britain?

Which came from overseas?

Are the imported foods on the rich or poor person's menu? Why?

Ask your grandparents who drank wine or beer when they were young...rich or poor?

Are any of the foods which we do not eat in Britain today eaten in other parts of the Roman empire?

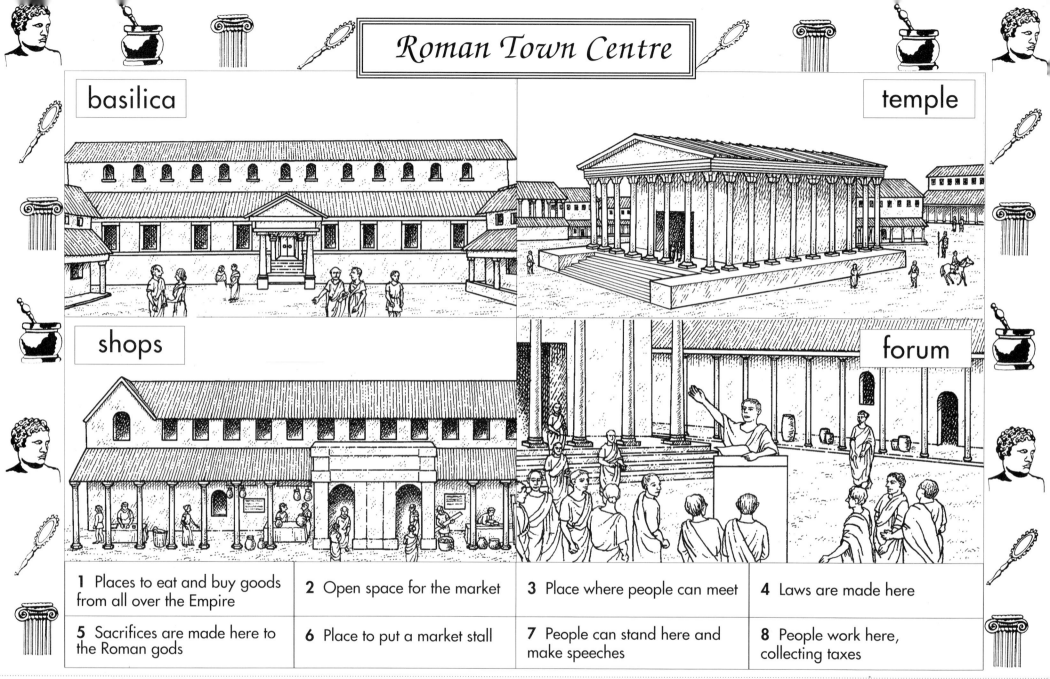

Town and Country

Background Information

Education
Children's education depended on the wealth of their families. Many poorer children never learnt to read or write. Up to the age of 12, children learnt simple arithmetic and to read and write in Latin. Most were educated by an older slave at home, but some went to primary school (ludus). Girls finished school at 12 and remained in the home, where they were taught to spin, weave and 'be ladies' by their mothers and female slaves. This prepared them for an arranged marriage, which could take place as early as 12. A small number of boys went to secondary school (schola), where they learnt Latin, philosophy, astronomy, geography, history, music and public speaking. This was a preparation for a career as a politician or lawyer. Local accents were discouraged. Some slaves received an education so that they could help with the schooling of the children in their care.

Villa Life
Roman country houses were known as villas. Some were simple farm cottages, others consisted of several buildings. Large villas were built around a courtyard. The walls were made of flint and mortar, and the roofs of tiles or slates. Around the courtyard were living rooms, bedrooms, a bathroom, a kitchen, storerooms and rooms for the slaves. There were also barns, stables and workshops. The villa was heated by a hypocaust. The floors of the best rooms were tiled with mosaics and the walls were plastered and painted with scenes from everyday life, myths and legends, gods and goddesses.

Farming methods were refined with the introduction of oxen, an improved corn-drying oven heated by a furnace, and new crops such as millet, rye, oats, flax, carrots, peas, celery, vines, plums, mulberry and walnuts.

Rural Life
The children could use the site drawing (page 46) of a villa and/or personal research to compile a list of jobs in and around the villa. The results could be compared with the Celtic site (page 36) and deductions made about similarities and differences, continuity and change. Comparisons could be made with a modern farm.

	Celtic	Roman	Modern
Rural home	hut	villa	farmhouse
Tools			

Comparing Town and Country
The children can compare town and country jobs. Which needed an education?

The children can find out what was involved in each of the town jobs. Which jobs have changed the most – town or country?

Town jobs

Architect
Surveyor
Builder

Lawyer
Politician
Baker

Butcher
Baker
Jeweller

Shoemaker
Weaver
Dyer

Points for Discussion
- What did girls do at 12?
- What did it mean to be 'ladies'?
- Why were the girls taught differently?
- Relate the different treatment to adult roles in Roman society.

The children could plan, design and make wax (Plasticine) tablets, a stylus and oil lamps. Discuss the modern equivalents to all three. Compare today with both Roman and Victorian times (slate, slate pencil and oil lamps). Why did Roman children use wax tablets and not papyrus or parchment? [Consider the cost – wax tablets are re-usable.]

Reconstruct a Roman Classroom
- Make up sums using Roman numerals (see page 56).
- Give a two-minute speech on an interest or chosen topic: for example, 'Why slavery is a good thing'.
- Re-write the story of Romulus and Remus on a scroll.
- Write the Roman alphabet on a wax tablet.

Silchester: A Roman Town

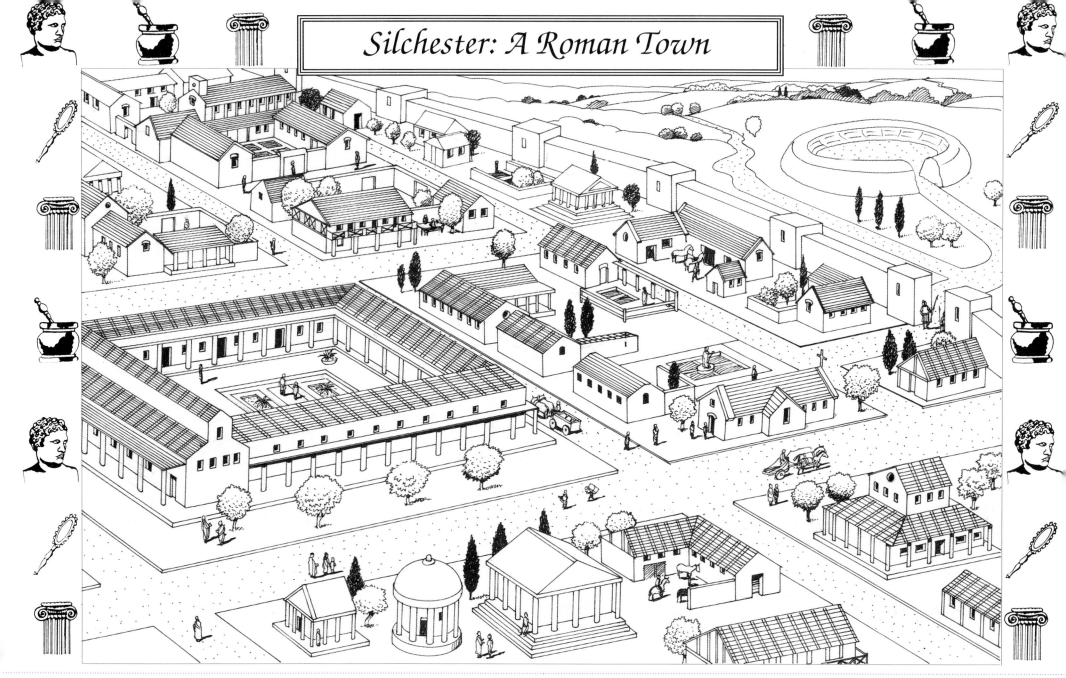

Teacher's notes. *Mask these notes before photocopying this sheet for the children.*
- The site plan can be enlarged for a wall display. The children should find out about particular buildings in a Romano-British town and present information around the display.
- Compare with a modern British town, using oblique aerial photographs.
- Look at such aspects as street planning, position and size of buildings, and transport.
- The children should consider why Roman towns in Britain were walled.

ROMAN ROADS 45

BACKGROUND INFORMATION

Prior to Roman engineering, the only roads in Britain were earth tracks. These generally traversed hills above the treeline. In contrast, the Romans constructed a network of straight roads to link their towns. The primary purpose of these roads was military transportation, in order to control and protect the empire. The roads also provided access to local markets and a distribution network throughout the empire. They helped to extend the generation of taxes, law enforcement and communication, hence they were well maintained.

When planning a road, Roman surveyors looked for the shortest, straightest, flattest route. To find this, they used various methods including lighting fires, flares or beacons, observing carrier pigeons or using a groma. The latter was a pair of boards fastened to form a cross. Lines with weights were hung from each corner. The surveyor obtained a straight line by looking through them.

The route having been planned, trees and turf were cleared and a deep trench dug and filled with layers of local stone. This solid base was covered with small stones or tiles and the surface covered with gravel or cobbles, which were tamped down. The surface was built with a raised curve, called a camber, to effect drainage into side ditches (and to increase visibility for a travelling army).

Write a story about a journey along a Roman road. Consider:
- Why are you travelling?
- Whom you might see?
- What happens to you?

Why was the building of roads important?

User	Importance for them
army	
farmers	
tax collectors	
governors	
the Empire	

CONSTRUCTING A ROMAN ROAD

Plan, design and make a model of a road and test it for drainage. Make working models of transport to travel on the road. Consult local maps for evidence of Roman roads in your area.

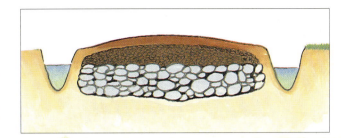

A Roman Villa

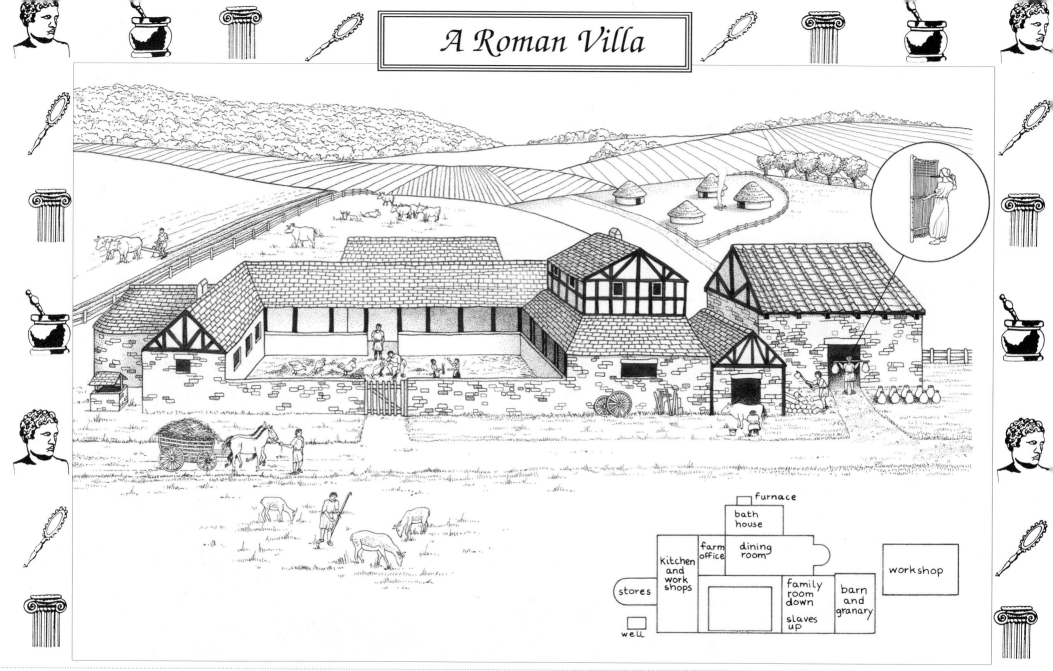

Teacher's notes. *Mask these notes before photocopying this sheet for the children.*
- As well as considering similarities and differences with the Celtic site on page 36, comparisons could be made with a farm today. The children should identify continuity and change: for example, growing crops (continuity), types of crop (change). Personal research would enhance this task.

- The site drawing could be enlarged for wall display. The children could identify the function of buildings using the plan.
- Look carefully at the activities taking place in and around the villa. Consider self-sufficiency. How do these activities meet the needs and wants of the family living in the villa? Why might they go to the town?

ROMAN BUILDINGS

47

BACKGROUND INFORMATION

Archaeologists have discovered many sites of Roman towns in Britain. These towns shared distinct features which were common throughout the empire. Careful planning ensured continuity of style and function.

Around the town was a wall. Initially, this was built in earth and clay but later in stone. There were four main gates or entrances to the town.

At the nucleus of any town was the forum or market place. It was normally built at the point where two main streets crossed. On three sides of the forum were covered walkways which contained shops, cafes and offices. On the fourth side was a basilica, a large building used as a law court and for other public functions. The town council (the ordo) met there.

The forum was at the centre of town life. People met, travelling entertainers performed and traders set up their temporary stalls there. This was also the place where public speaking and debate occurred.

Specific Roman architectural styles and features could be found throughout towns both in Britain and the rest of the empire. Of these, the most notable are the arches, columns, mosaics, statues and wall paintings.

The building materials used included both stone and concrete. Concrete was made by combining lime mortar with marble chippings and stones. The concrete slurry was formed in wooden moulds. When set, it formed a homogeneous mass. The final surface of concrete was rough and unattractive, so a facing of marble, stone slab or baked brick was added.

The policy of deliberate town planning helped the Romans to impose control over the previously scattered tribes of Celtic Britain. The town became a focus of local life.

BUILDINGS TODAY

The children should have the opportunity to find out about buildings in their own town in order to help them identify differences between the past and the present. This could include designing a computer-generated data-collection sheet to collate information on the site, location, function and appearance of the following: town hall, market place(s), places of worship, shops, cafes, law or magistrate's court. Photographs of these features will support effective classroom activities.

Match photographs to location.

BUILDINGS IN ROMAN BRITAIN

Use the Activity Sheet on page 42 to identify types of building and their uses in a Roman town. The children can locate the pictures on page 42 on the oblique view on page 44

MAKING COMPARISONS

The children can record in a variety of ways.

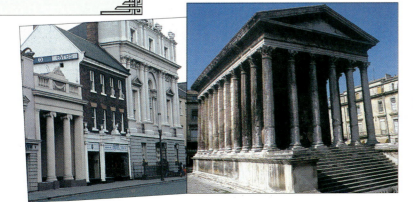

Identify continuity and change.

Identify similarities and differences.

Roman Britain

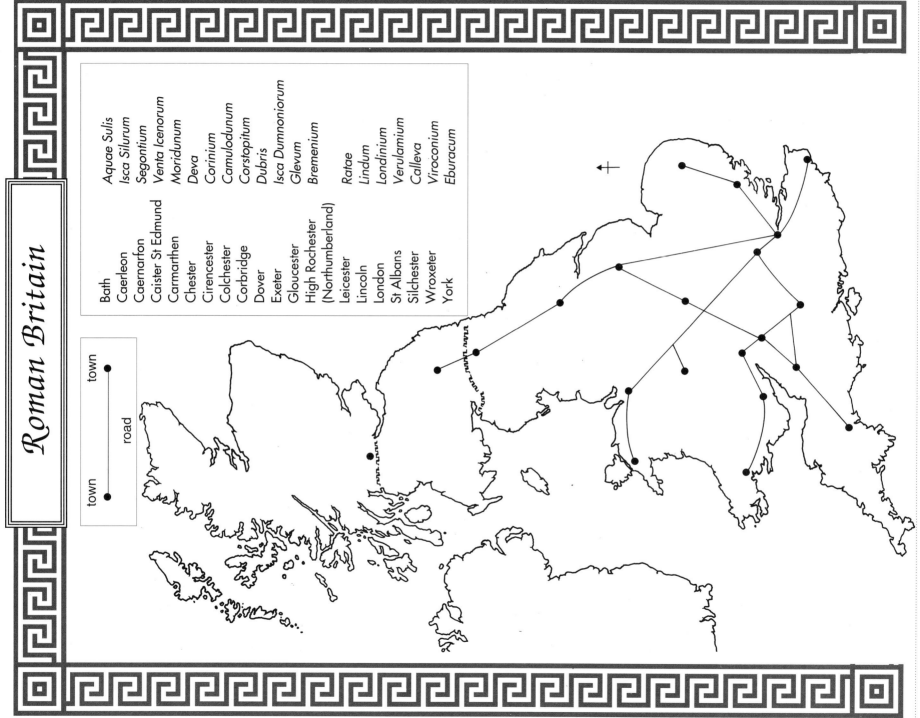

Bath	Aquae Sulis
Caerleon	Isca Silurum
Caernarfon	Segontium
Caister St Edmund	Venta Icenorum
Carmarthen	Moridunum
Chester	Deva
Cirencester	Corinium
Colchester	Camulodunum
Corbridge	Corstopitum
Dover	Dubris
Exeter	Isca Dumnoniorum
Gloucester	Glevum
High Rochester (Northumberland)	Bremenium
Leicester	Ratae
Lincoln	Lindum
London	Londinium
St Albans	Verulamium
Silchester	Calleva
Wroxeter	Viroconium
York	Eburacum

● town ——— town road

Teacher's Notes. *Mask these notes before photocopying this sheet for the children.*
The map could be enlarged on a photocopier.
- Using an atlas, the children should try to identify the places shown and mark their names on this map.
- The teacher could mask the Roman names in the key and ask the children to research them.
- The children could plan a journey from one town to another and decide which road to use. They could find the names of the Roman roads.
- Identify the Roman town and road nearest to your school.

TRADE AND INDUSTRY

49

IMPORTS
Give the children a list of products which the Romans received from their empire. Ask them to find out which parts of the empire they came from.

Using a 'boat' outline to represent each country, the children place the 'boats' on a map.

POTTERY
During the first 100 years of Roman Britain, samian ware (a reddish-brown pottery) was imported from Gaul, mainly for the rich. Samian pottery was decorated by pressing soft clay into a carved mould. After the mould had been removed, extra clay was added to form a rim. Later British potters (in the New Forest and Northamptonshire) favoured the wheel-turned pot, to which decoration was applied freehand. The black, unglazed pottery called Belgic black was copied by British potters. Many museums have excellent examples.

Discuss with the children who has a 'best' set of pots at home. Establish the cost of everyday plates and 'best'. The children could use an old mail-order catalogue. Many Romans had a similar practice. Poorer people used cheap pottery all the time.

Working in groups, the children should try to reproduce samian and black pottery. Which is more difficult? Which takes longer to make? Why would one cost more than the other?

MONEY
What do coins tell us?

Date issued

Latin for 'To the glory of God Queen'

Image of monarch

Image of emperor

Name of monarch

Whether the monarch is first with that name

Name of emperor

Roman coins were a source of information. They showed the people of the empire what the reigning emperor looked like (often flattering). The reverse might depict a victory or fashions. (Hadrian created the fashion of men wearing beards.)

Name of country: Britannia

Britannia armed and on guard at Hadrian's Wall, keeping watch over the northern edge of the empire

LOOKING FOR CLUES
Make a collection of Roman and modern coins. *History 1: Resource Pack* contains replica coins. Find out more about a person on a coin.

The chart lists the coins in order of value.

| ROMAN COINS ||
Metal	Name
bronze	as
bronze	sestertius
silver/copper	denarius
gold	aures

ASKING QUESTIONS

In which way are Roman/modern coins the same/different?

What were the coins used for? What does this tell us about Roman times?

Can the children sequence the Roman coins? What fashion changes can they see?

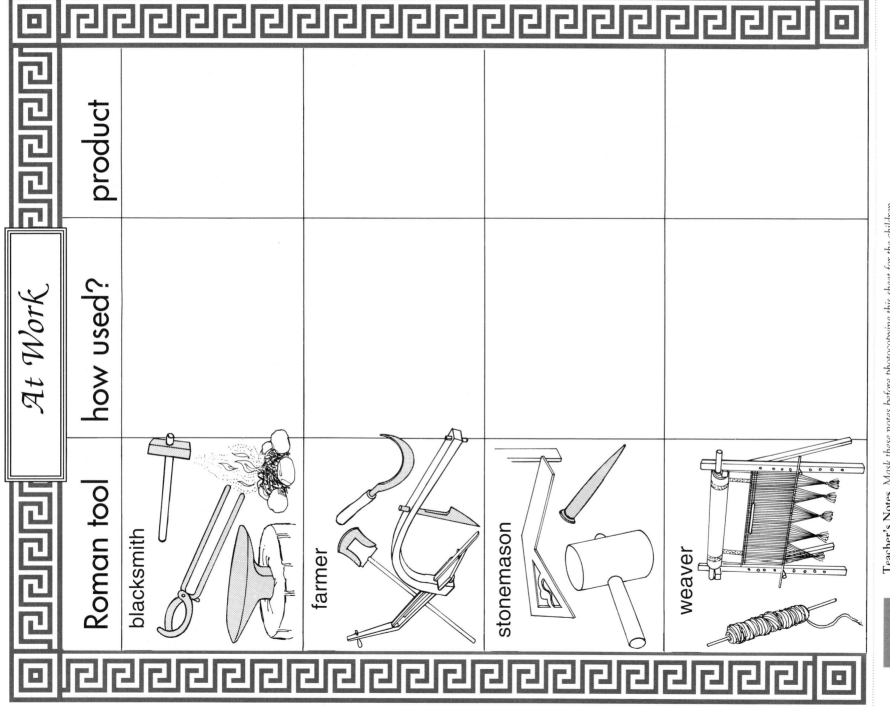

At Work

Roman tool	how used?	product
blacksmith		
farmer		
stonemason		
weaver		

Teacher's Notes. *Mask these notes before photocopying this sheet for the children.*
This sheet could be enlarged on a photocopier.
Only a small range is covered here of the specialist crafts common in Roman Britain. Similar activities can be developed based on carpentry, the work of potters etc. Books and other illustrative materials should be available for reference, to augment the evidence provided here.
- The children could write about, or draw, how each tool would be used. (Middle column)
- The product column may include obvious connections, such as a sword from the blacksmith, a headstone from the mason, to less obvious products, such as wheat from the plough.
- Using pictures of everyday life, the children could identify each product with a particular craft.

Religious Life 51

Background Information

Prior to the arrival of the Romans, a variety of religious practices existed amongst the various Celtic tribes. A different god was attributed to each aspect of everyday life.

The Romans brought to Britain their own state religion, which was significantly influenced by Greek beliefs: for example, the Greek god Zeus had become Jupiter. Roman belief had two main strands: spirits (*numina*) which were domestic guardians and were worshipped in the home; and gods and goddesses exalted at public ceremonies. Central to Roman religion was belief in the emperor himself. Deification normally took place after death. Some emperors proclaimed themselves living gods – a means of political control.

As conquerors, the Romans generally tolerated existing local religions (provided they upheld the worship of the emperor and gods). They synthesised Celtic gods with their own: for instance, Sulis Minerva was a combination of the Celtic Sul and the Roman goddess Minerva.

Individual temples honoured a particular god, goddess or emperor: for example, the Temple of Claudius at Camulodunum (Colchester). Temples were not intended for congregational worship but public ceremony, including sacrifices of animals and offerings of food by priests. Everyday worship took place in the home and included sacrifices to the gods of the household.

Superstition had great influence over everyday life. A bulla was a simple knotted leather purse (or a chain, if from a wealthy family) worn around the neck, containing a golden globe with a protective amulet inside. Natural phenomena, such as flocks of birds and lightning, were considered to be omens from the gods. Priests disembowelled animals; the shape of the liver or blemishes on it indicated the attitudes of the gods. Astrologers told fortunes by examining the position of the stars at the time of people's birth. The throwing of dice and the reading of palms were common practices.

Various religious ceremonies included a wide range of burial customs. The two main methods were cremation and inhumation. A funeral could be an elaborate undertaking. The deceased was placed on a couch with feet towards the door, so that the spirits could exit.

Torches and candles, along with pine cones, would be burned to disguise the smell of the body. A coin was placed in the dead person's mouth. This was payment for the boatman who rowed the soul across the River of the Dead. If the deceased had been important, the body was carried on a litter by slaves. Hired mourners, to emphasise the grief, accompanied the family and were followed by flute players. Notables were placed in the forum and speeches made in their honour. Burial took place outside the town walls. When the was body cremated, the ashes were placed in an urn with the personal possessions required in the 'next life'. The grave (sarcophagus) was marked with an upright stone on which appeared the name, parentage, career, age at death and notable achievements of the interned. The inscription was painted in red. The poor were normally buried in communal tombs.

Although tolerant, the Romans would persecute any groups refusing to worship their gods. Jews, Christians and Druids were exclusive in their beliefs, so the Romans persecuted them. After three centuries of persecution, Christianity was officially tolerated by the decree of the Emperor Constantine. When the Emperor Theodosius was baptised, it became the state religion.

Romans and Omens

Collect and record data on superstitions then and now. The teacher could relate the funeral ceremony to a group of children (see opposite). Through illustrations or drama sketches, the children present the order of the ceremony (reproduction artefacts as props).

Points for Discussion

- How did the Romans treat the Christians?
- Why did they treat them this way?
- Why did their attitude change?

Gods and Goddesses

The children could research these gods and find visual images of each. Using their knowledge of everyday life, the children could make deductions about who might pray to each god (a farmer to Ceres for fine weather, for example). Through personal research, the children should find out about other Roman gods.

JUNO (Women and marriage)

JUPITER (father of the Gods)

NEPTUNE (sea)

BACCHUS (wine and celebration)

MINERVA (wisdom)

CERES (corn)

VENUS (love)

MARS (war)

Evidence in Stone

Teacher's Notes. *Mask these notes before photocopying this sheet for the children.*
The evidence shows: A bust of Julius Caesar. A statue of Claudius 1. The butcher's shop and the children at play reflect everyday life. These could be used separately.
Ask the children to:
- Suggest reasons why people had statues/busts carved?
- What evidence is there for similarity and difference between now and then?

Children should recognise that sources help answer questions about the past. Provide questions, some of which can be answered from these sources, others which cannot, for example: Can you list three games children played. [cannot] What did a butcher shop sell? [can] Add an additional source, for example, page 54. Can they answer such questions when drawing on additional historical sources.

- The picture of Claudius shows him as a god. Raise the question 'Was Claudius a man or a god?' Discuss with the children that, if this is the only source used, how might deficiencies in evidence lead them to an inadequate interpretation of the past, for example, how men dressed.

Art and Architecture

Commemorating Events

Statues, plaques and other memorials have been erected by people throughout the centuries and in all parts of the world to commemorate famous people and events. They are a primary source and help us to answer questions about the past. There will be monuments of some kind within easy reach of all schools. The children should visit these or use photographs of them.

Asking Questions

What is it?

When was it built?

Who built it?

Why was it built?

What does it tell us about the person/event?

Why was it important for people to remember?

Collect photographs of famous statues in Britain which were built at different times. Raise similar questions and reinforce the idea that people in the past have erected these for future generations, to communicate what they deemed important. They tell us about the values of people in the past. The children should put the photographs in chronological order.

The Roman Legacy

The Romans bequeathed a rich variety of evidence, which helps us to understand their time.

Monumental arches commemorated famous victories. Claudius had one erected in Rome to mark his conquest of Britain.

Statues of real people and the gods.

Bas-reliefs depicting scenes from famous events and everyday life.

Inscriptions also reflecting the great and the commonplace.

Mosaics containing myth and reality.

Looking at Roman Buildings

Using pictures of Roman buildings, the children should recognise and name:

Arches

The arch was used not only as a structural element in buildings and bridges but also as a monument to commemorate victories. To build an arch, a semi-circular wooden frame was made on which were set wedge-shaped blocks of stone (voussoirs). When the last stone (the keystone) was inserted in the crown of the arch, the frame was removed.

Columns

The Romans further developed the Greek column.

Mosaics

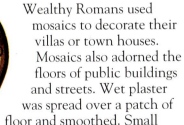

Wealthy Romans used mosaics to decorate their villas or town houses. Mosaics also adorned the floors of public buildings and streets. Wet plaster was spread over a patch of floor and smoothed. Small cubes or irregular-shaped fragments of glass, glazed pottery or marble were laid close together on the wet plaster and slightly pressed in. When the laying was finished, the joints were filled with plaster.

Make Mosaics

Mosaics often depicted classical tales. Read the Romulus and Remus story to the children (page 59). They could make mosaics which re-tell the sequence of events. Tile, paper, clay, seeds, beads can be used to create effective displays.

Be an Architect: Reconstruct the Past

Give the children a plan of a Roman forum. By photocopying or drawing to scale, they can:
• Enlarge the plan several times and then build a three-dimensional model on the enlarged plan.
• Write about the activities which took place in each area of the forum. This could be factual or creative writing based on personal research: for example, an account of a travelling actor visiting the forum.

Plan of a Forum

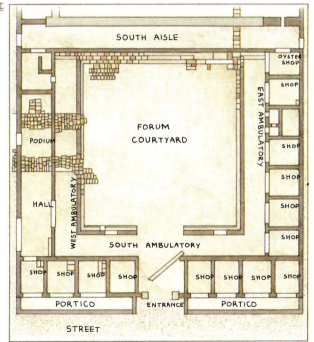

Children at Play

 Teacher's notes. *Mask these notes before photocopying this sheet for the children.*
- Ask the children what types of play would take place with these toys.
- The children can record from what materials the games are made. Compare with toys and games today.
- The children should describe how they think the game was played. (Deficiencies in evidence may lead to different interpretations.)
What are today's equivalents?
- Using knowledge gained from work on 'People', 'Buildings', 'Entertainment' and their own research, the children could produce a diary/wall display on 'A day in the life of a Roman child'.
- Give the children a range of statements for example: 'Roman children played with dolls'. 'Their favourite game was 'leap frog'. Can the children identify which is fact and which is point of view?
- Evidence of children at play depicts 'Roman children'. Ask the children why there is little evidence of the play activities of British children in Roman times. What games and toys might they have enjoyed? Is our view guesswork or based on evidence?

Entertainment and Leisure

Background Information

The public baths were the social centre of every Roman town. All sections of society could be found there. Wealthy people went daily with their slaves. Separate rooms were available for men and women, and smaller baths had separate times for each. The baths were not only a place for cleaning but also for keeping fit and socialising.

There were several rooms in the public baths. Having changed in the first room, the visitor went outside into the courtyard to exercise. This might have included wrestling, skipping and running. Beginning to sweat, the visitor moved to the warm room (tepidarium), followed by an even hotter room (caldarium) for anyone who could stand it. An attendant rubbed olive oil into the body and then scraped off the surplus with a tool made from metal or ivory (called a strigil). Afterwards, the visitor went to the cool room (frigidarium), where he/she might have a massage, a swim in the plunge pool, a chat to friends or food and drink. Communal toilets were available. Some baths were sited at hot springs. The Romans believed the natural hot water to be sacred and to have the power to heal.

The second most popular entertainment was the amphitheatre. Here, gladiators and animals fought while spectators gambled on the results. Britain did not have stone-seated amphitheatres such as the Colosseum in Rome. In Britain, they were much smaller with wooden seats.

Nearly every Romano-British town would have had a theatre for plays, dancing, mimes and concerts. These shows were financed by wealthy citizens, as free entry could gain the favour of the ordinary townsfolk.

Chariot races in Roman Britain were held in fields, watched by spectators on wooden seats. The chariots were like carts pulled by teams of two, three, four or eight horses, with each race lasting seven laps (or 5 km). Accidents were frequent, especially at the turns. Charioteers carried daggers to free themselves from tangled reins.

Going to the Baths
Introduce the Roman habit of bathing by asking the children about their experiences of bathing. Ask the children to conduct a survey.

Design a Questionnaire
Children can compare their findings with practice in Roman times.

Bathing
Why?
keep clean	relax	fun	exercise	safety
Where?
shower	bath	seaside	swimming baths	sauna
When?
each day	once a week	only on holiday

Entertainment in the Amphitheatre
Ask the children to find out what entertainments took place in the amphitheatre. They can be creative in the presentation of their findings: for example, big book, wall display, scroll, DTP.

The children should consider how the Romans would know about events at the amphitheatre. Discussion might include the fact that newspapers, TV and posters were not available then but that the forum provided a meeting place and a point for information.

Role Play
The children should use photographs and pictures (see *History 1: Resource Pack*) to consider why and how Roman baths were used. Imaginary interviews could be conducted.

Children
Children in Roman Britain played outdoor games. These included ancient equivalents of wrestling, fencing and bowling the hoop. Ball games were particularly popular, especially trigon (throwing a hard leather ball between three people) and harpastum, which was similar to rugby. Children also played with dolls. Many kept pets, mainly dogs.

Board Games
Board games were very popular with children and adults. Many included the use of a die and counter. A game similar to draughts was played and there was a variety of gambling, including dice rolling.

At the Races
Brainstorm with the children the dangers of chariot racing. They can then plan, design and make a chariot race board which reflects these dangers, for example 'crushed chariot = out of game' or 'stuck in the mud = miss a go'. Consider using Roman numerals on the boards and dice.

Roman Numerals

I	1	XI	11	XXX	30
II	2	XII	12	XL	40
III	3	XIII	13	L	50
IV	4	XIV	14	LX	60
V	5	XV	15	LXX	70
VI	6	XVI	16	LXXX	80
VII	7	XVII	17	XC	90
VIII	8	XVIII	18	C	100
IX	9	XIX	19	D	500
X	10	XX	20	M	1000

Write the Roman numerals for:
2 ☐   7 ☐   9 ☐
17 ☐   19 ☐   20 ☐
50 ☐   100 ☐   500 ☐

Write the Arabic numerals for:
X ☐   XIII ☐   XIX ☐
C ☐   M ☐   XC ☐

Write the Roman numerals for:
24 ☐   32 ☐   51 ☐

Write the Arabic numerals for:
MC ☐   DXC ☐

Write your date of birth in words
....

in Arabic numerals ....

in Roman numerals ....

Make up some sums for a friend using Roman numerals

Teacher's notes. *Mask these notes before photocopying this sheet for the children.*
• The children could work out several different dates: for example, today, family birthdays, friends' birthdays.

• Find examples of the use of Roman numerals (a) today and (b) on Roman artefacts (for example, a milestone).

LEGACY 57

Introduce the idea of 'legacy' in terms of how the past is still with us today. The focus may be on the Roman legacy but the idea of a continuing and varied legacy should be explored: for example, Roman months but mainly Norse days, Roman numerals but the Hindu symbol for zero.

ROMAN NUMBER SYSTEM
The Romans used seven letters, separately and in combination, to represent all their numbers:
I (1)   V (5)   X (10)   L (50)   C (100)
D (500)   M (1000)

Addition and subtraction are used to make numbers from groupings of these seven letters. A number on the left of a higher number is subtracted; a number on its right is added. For example,

four = IV = 5 minus 1
six = VI = 5 plus 1
nine = IX = 10 minus 1
eleven = XI = 10 plus 1

The Activity Sheet on page 56 will help the children understand the system.

LOOK AROUND FOR EVIDENCE
• Coins
• Datestones
• Pages in a book (introduction/appendices often have Roman folios
• Churches
• Mottos
• Clocks

LANGUAGE
Latin was the common language of educated people until the late Middle Ages. Until within living memory, it was the language of the Roman Catholic liturgy.

WORDS DERIVED FROM LATIN		
circus	pendulum	exit
miser	agenda	giant
recipe	album	victory
fungus	sponge	school
genius	lavatory	street

Give the children the above words, ask them to find their meanings and use them correctly in a sentence.

LATIN	MEANING	DERIVATIVE
liber	book	library
omnibus	all	bus
magister	master	magistrate
video	see	video
radius	beam	radio

The children could be given a Latin word and asked to work out a derivative. The meaning might give them a clue.

Look at coins in use today and pre-decimal coins. The children could investigate the Latin words and numbers.

CALENDAR
The early Roman calendar was reformed by Julius Caesar in 46 BC. The Julian Calendar contained 365 days with 366 days every fourth year. Because of its cumulative innacuracy, it was it was replaced by the Gregorian calendar (Pope Gregory XIII) from 1582 onwards but not in Britain until 1752.

MONTH	LATIN ORIGIN	
January	After Janus, the god who looked both ways with his two faces	
February	After Februa, festival of purification	
March	After Mars, the god of war	
April	After Aprilis	
May	After Maia, an earth goddess	
June	After Junius, a popular female name	
July	After Julius Caesar	
August	After Augustus	
September	Septem (7) Seventh	*Months of the ancient Roman year*
October	Octem (8) Eighth	
November	Novem (9) Ninth	
December	Decem (10) Tenth	

The children could write their birth year or month: for example, MCMLX or 'I was born in Maia's month'.

Teacher's notes. *Mask these notes before photocopying this sheet for the children.*
The picture sequence can be used in several ways.
- The page may be enlarged on their photocopier.
- The children could sequence the pictures and use them to help to retell the story.
- They should be encouraged to think about point of view by filling in the speech bubbles. Who might have said what and why?
- They could use the pictures to write a play which is acted before an audience.
- They could draw their own picture sequence for the historical development of Rome.

The Origins of Rome

The story of Romulus and Remus

A beautiful princess was kept prisoner by her uncle so that she could not marry and have children. Her uncle had stolen the throne from her father and made himself king. The uncle was frightened that the princess would have a baby son who would take back the throne when he grew up.

But Mars, the Roman god of war, secretly married the princess. She gave birth to twin boys Romulus and Remus. When the wicked uncle heard of the birth, he was very angry. He ordered a servant to drown the twins in the River Tiber.

The two babies were carried to the river, but the servant could not kill them. Instead, he put them in a basket and let them float away down the river, hoping that they would not drown.

The basket went ashore near seven hills.

The babies lay there for some time. Then a she-wolf crept from the nearby bushes, sniffing the air. She could smell the twins. Slowly, she crawled towards the basket and looked in. The twins cried because they were hungry. The wolf fed the twins and lay with them to keep them warm until a shepherd came.

Romulus and Remus grew up with the shepherd and his wife. When they reached manhood, they searched out the wicked uncle and took the throne away from him.

Romulus and Remus decided to build a city where they were first found by the wolf. But they could not agree on which hill to build it. Remus chose the top of one hill and Romulus the top of another. They agreed that the first one to see a vulture could decide. But they argued again when each said he had seen the vulture first.

They argued about who should be the ruler of the new city. They started to fight. Romulus drew his sword and killed his twin brother Remus.

Romulus went with a small band of followers and built the city which we call Rome.

Beginnings

About 25 kilometres from the sea, the River Tiber passes a group of seven hills. These hills were a good place to settle. The land was fertile. Crops could be easily grown and sheep raised. Also, it was too far from the sea for pirates to attack.

Settlers built small villages on the seven hills. The people of these villages worked together and the area grew in power and importance. These were the first Romans. One of their kings was Romulus.

Etruscans from the north came to live alongside the Romans. The Etruscans were excellent soldiers and engineers, and so the power of Rome grew. Eventually, Etruscan kings ruled Rome. Rome traded with cities far and wide. In 507 BC the Roman people threw out their Etruscan leaders and once again ruled themselves.

 Teacher's notes. *Mask these notes before photocopying this sheet for the children.*
- The story is myth. 'Beginnings' is a factual account based on current evidence. Encourage the children to distinguish between myth and reality.
- Read the story of Romulus and Remus with the children. Are there parts of the story they find hard to believe? Why?
- Read 'Beginnings' with the children. Are there parts which they find hard to believe?
- Think about similarities and differences between the story and 'Beginnings'.
- Discuss other myths and legends. Why do we enjoy them?
- Why did people in the past not have the factual accounts we have today? Consider his point of view. Do they agree with him? Why?

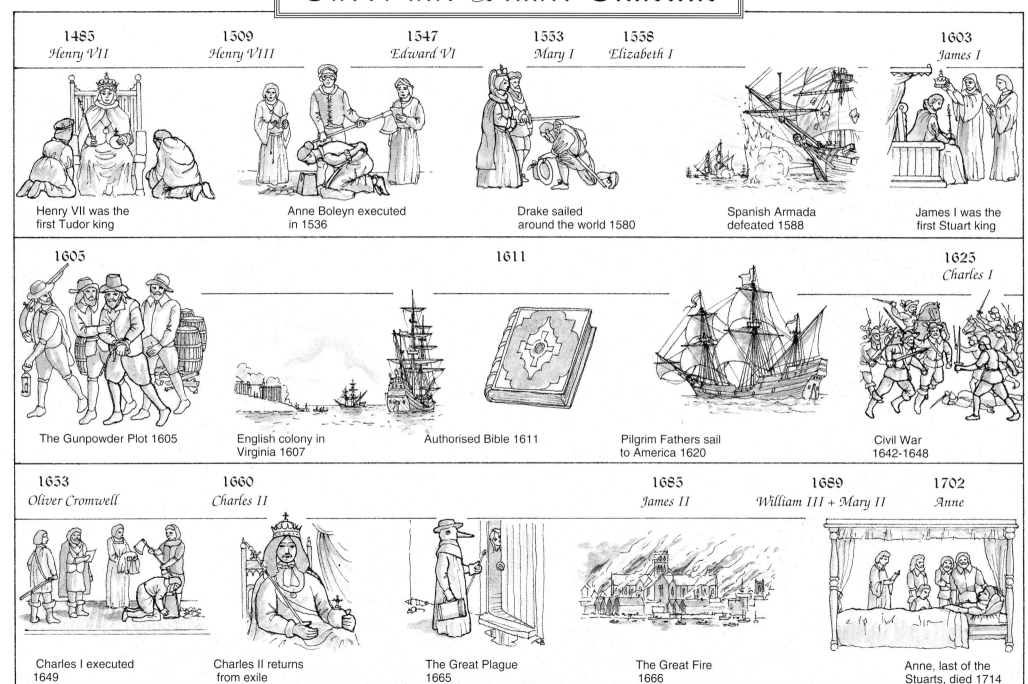

TUDOR AND STUART TIMES

BACKGROUND INFORMATION

The Tudor and Stuart period began just over 500 years ago at the end of the Middle Ages, when Henry Tudor, a member of the Welsh branch of the Tudor family, was crowned. He was the first Tudor monarch. The period ended at the beginning of the 18th century, when Queen Anne I, the last Stuart ruler, died.

These two ruling dynasties – the English Tudors and the Scottish Stuarts – presided over one of the most fascinating and turbulent periods in British history.

It was a time of much conflict and persecution. There were quarrels and bitterness between the Crown and Parliament, between Catholics and Protestants, and between England and foreign powers. There were no fewer than 12 rulers, including four of the best-known monarchs in English history – Henry VIII, Elizabeth I, Charles I and Charles II – and Oliver Cromwell, England's first and only uncrowned ruler.

There were important changes in the way England was governed, in forms of worship and in building. Trade, the arts and the sciences flourished, and the explorers of the day discovered lands unknown to Europeans.

The Tudor and Stuart period has provided some of the more famous 'stories' from history: Drake's game of bowls on Plymouth Ho as the Armada sailed by, Raleigh's gallantry as he laid his cloak over the puddle which blocked his queen's path, and the apple which fell on Isaac Newton's head. Although these popular perceptions of history need not be avoided, it is important to look carefully for any historical evidence to support them. There may be some accuracy in terms of the characters and locations involved in such stories, but much of the content is more often legend than totally reliable historical information.

	HISTORY												
ATTAINMENT TARGETS	1								2		3		
LEVELS	2			3			4			2	3	4	2	3	4
STATEMENTS	a	b	c	a	b	c	a	b	c	a	a	a	a	a	a
60 Timeline			•	•	•	•	•	•	•	•	•	•	•	•	•
61 Tudor and Stuart times											•	•		•	•
62 The Tree of Succession	•			•	•	•			•					•	•
63 Tudor and Stuart rulers	•			•	•	•			•					•	•
64 A feast fit for a king			•				•							•	
65 Life at court			•				•	•						•	•
66 A Stuart menu			•				•							•	•
67 The break with Rome		•		•			•							•	•
68 Roundheads and Cavaliers	•			•			•							•	•
69 Civil War and Restoration			•					•	•					•	•
70 The death warrant of Charles I				•				•						•	•
71 Portraits of the rulers			•							•	•			•	•
72 Travelling in Tudor and Stuart times		•	•								•			•	•
73 Towns, trade and transport			•				•	•						•	•
74 Living through the Plague	•	•												•	•
75 The Great Plague		•	•											•	•
76 Extracts from Samuel Pepys's Diary	•													•	•
77 London's burning	•	•	•											•	•
78 Religious changes			•	•	•									•	•
79 James I and religion			•	•	•									•	•
80 Treason and plot	•			•		•								•	•
81 Exploration and empire		•	•	•										•	•
82 Views of women			•	•										•	•
83 Famous people and their legacies			•					•						•	•

There are numerous places to visit which have links with the Tudors and Stuarts. You may be lucky enough to live near a Tudor or Stuart residence, building, ship, monument or historical site, where there may be a wealth of artefacts such as furniture, costumes, weapons, paintings and household objects for the children to look at and handle. A visit to one of these places could stimulate work on the study unit or be used to conclude the topic. Some have education officers willing to support teachers in their work by providing teachers' packs, other forms of information and perhaps opportunities for role play. A local museum may have replica costumes for the children to try on. Secondary sources of evidence, such as reference books, will still be a mainstay in teaching this unit.

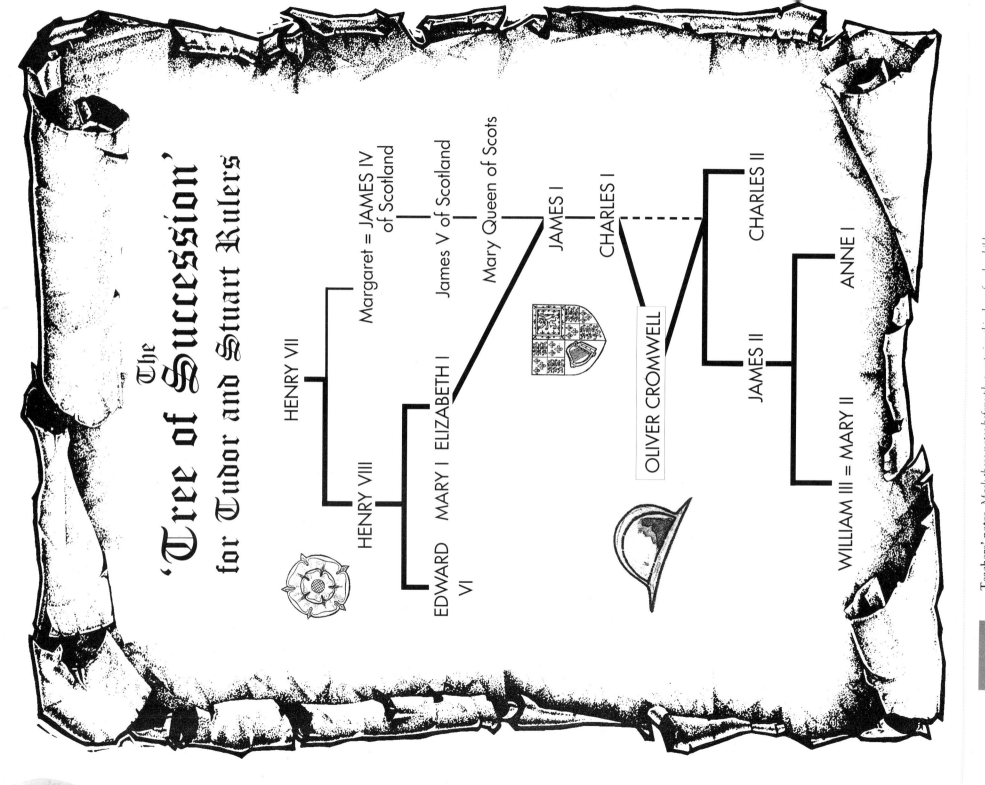

Tudor and Stuart Rulers

Background Information

Apart from the ten years of the Commonwealth, England was ruled from 1485 to 1714 by members of the English House of Tudor followed by members of the Scottish House of Stuart.

The first of the Tudor line, Henry, was crowned King Henry VII (1485-1509). By his marriage, he united the two feuding families of Lancaster and York, and the Wars of the Roses ended.

After Henry's death, his younger son succeeded to the throne as Henry VIII (1509-1547). Although Henry VIII married six times, only three children outlived him. Henry's only son was crowned King Edward VI (1547-1553) when his father died. As he was still a child, England and Wales were governed for him by a council of noblemen. Edward, a strict Protestant, was a sickly boy who died at the age of 16. He was succeeded by his elder sister Mary, a staunch Catholic, who became Queen Mary I (1553-1558).

As Mary died childless, her younger half-sister Elizabeth inherited the throne: Queen Elizabeth I (1558-1603). Elizabeth never married, so when she died the Tudor dynasty died out too. The throne passed to her Protestant cousin, James VI of Scotland, who was crowned James I of England (1603-1625), thus uniting the thrones of the two countries. James was the first of the Stuart dynasty in England.

After James I's death, his younger son became King Charles I (1625-1649). His frequent quarrels with Parliament led to the Civil War (1642-1648) and ultimately to his execution for treason. England then became a republic known as the Commonwealth, ruled eventually by the Lord Protector, Oliver Cromwell (1653-1658). He was succeeded by his son, Richard, who resigned in 1660.

When Cromwell died, the elder son of Charles I was invited to return from exile to be crowned King Charles II (1660-1685). As Charles had no children when he died, the crown passed to his younger brother James II (1685-1688) who attempted to make England a Catholic country again. His unpopularity led to his exile when Parliament offered his Protestant daughter Mary and her husband, William of Orange, the throne as Mary II (1689-1694) and William III (1689-1702). After their deaths James II's younger daughter was crowned Queen Anne I, the last of the Stuart rulers (1702-1714).

Using the 'Tree of Succession'

The 'Tree of Succession' (page 62) can be used as the basis for a wall display. As the children find out about events in a particular reign, for example, Henry VIII's break with Rome, the ruler's portrait can be placed on the tree. If the events and personalities are dealt with in order, this will add to the children's understanding of chronology as they see the tree grow.

Use copies of the 'portrait cards' on page 71, or children's paintings or drawings of each ruler, to put on the tree. Paint, or make a collage of, the Tudor Rose, the Stuart Coats of Arms and the Roundhead helmet. Use a word-processing program to print out labels for each picture.

Using the 'Portrait Cards'

Contemporaneous portraits are a useful source of evidence for developing AT 2: Interpretations of History. Children should understand that a portrait is not a totally accurate representation of a person. The image depends in part on the artist's view of the person. Some subjects insisted that their portrait was painted in a certain way.

Use the 'portrait cards' to encourage discussion about each ruler. What did they look like? What kind of expression do they have? What can you tell about their character? Compare and contrast the clothes and hair-style of one ruler with those of another and those of today.

Different portraits can give us different information about the person and the times they lived in. Compare the 'portrait cards' with other pictures which are available.

Photocopy sets of the 'portrait cards' on page 71. Cut off the names, mount the portraits on card and laminate. Make your own sets of matching 'title cards' which give the name and title of each ruler.

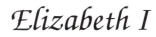

Use the cards to help the children become familiar with each ruler and to reinforce ideas of chronology.

Play 'Portrait Snap' with the picture cards by matching two Tudor or Stuart rulers. Later use both the 'portraits' and 'title' cards.

Sort the 'portrait cards' into Tudor and Stuart rulers. Who is the odd one out?

Build up mini 'family trees': for example, for the Tudors only. Help the children to recognise relationships such as grandfather, father, son, daughter, brother and sister.

Lay out the 'portrait' and 'title' cards to show the line of succession. Play 'Who's missing?' by removing one portrait/title pair at a time.

Once the whole 'tree of succession' has been built up, ask questions based on the display. For example: In Tudor and Stuart times, how many kings were there? How many queens? Who ruled as a child? Who was not a king or queen? Who was the first Tudor ruler? Who was the last? Who was the first Stuart ruler? Who was the last? Who ruled first Henry VII or Henry VIII?

A Feast Fit For a King

Notes of the Lords Diettes at Hoghton

at the Kinges beeing ther 1617

Sundaie dinner the xvijth of August 1617

The first course for the Lordes table

Salletes	pastie of venison hote	Capons roste
boyld capon	roste turkie	Sallett
mutton could	veale souced	beefe roste
boyld chickinges	Swan roste j & j for to morow	tong pye could
shoulder of mutton roste	chicking pye hote	force boyld
Duckes boyld	goose rosted	hearons roste could
loyne of veale rosted	Rabbettes could	Curlew pye could
Sallettes	Jiggites of ..... (hole) boyld	minct pye hote
hanch of venison roste	Tripe pye	Custardes
soucd capon	brestes of veale boyld	pigges roste

The second course

hote phesant j & j for the king	plouers	palletes of grease
quailes 6 for the king	Redd Deare pye	Dryed tongus
partridge	pigg souced	turkie pye
poulte	hote hearons roste 3 of a Dishe	phesant pye
Artichocke pye	Lambe roste	Lyed tarte
chickinges	gamons of bacon	hogges cheekes Dryed
Curlewes roste	pigeons roste	turkie chickes cold
pease buttered	made Dishe	St .... on
rabbettes	chicking souce	
Duckes	peare tarte	

Teacher's notes. *Mask these notes before photocopying this sheet for the children.*
Sallet=salad; force= a mixture of meat and herbs; soucd or souced=soused=sauced, seasoned, flavoured, pickled; lyed=mixed.

After tasting the roast beef, King James is said to have knighted it 'Sir Loin of Beef' because he enjoyed it so much. The name became today's 'sirloin of beef'.

LIFE AT COURT

BACKGROUND INFORMATION

The court of each Tudor and Stuart monarch had its own special features and style. Some of the most interesting evidence about court life to use with children comes from the reigns of Henry VIII, Elizabeth I and James I.

The court, which was in session wherever the king or queen stayed, was always a hive of activity. Affairs of state were conducted there, advisers and counsellors were available, explorers and sea captains paid visits, and playwrights and artists brought their latest works.

The lords and ladies of the court – courtiers – had to maintain high standards of dress and be able to afford to keep up with the lifestyle of the sovereign. Their clothes were extravagant and costly – rich fabrics in bright colours, heavily embroidered and jewelled.

The court was usually based at one of the magnificent royal palaces such as Hampton Court, Greenwich or Whitehall, many of which were surrounded by beautiful formal gardens, deer parks and forests. The palaces were lavishly decorated and furnished. Despite being the focus of government business, the emphasis at court was on enjoyment and entertainment, both indoors and outdoors. Courtiers would play cards, dice, chess, draughts and backgammon. They would sing, dance, play and listen to music. There would be riding, hawking and hunting, often accompanied by enormous picnics, jousting to watch and sports such as archery, wrestling and real tennis to take part in. At night, plays and masques (musical entertainments with drama, poems and dances) would be performed. There might be fireworks, poetry readings and jokes from the resident jester. Great banquets would take place.

Both Henry VIII and Elizabeth I moved from one palace to another with their courts, advisers and the royal household. This involved the movement of bedclothes, linen, furniture, kitchen equipment and large numbers of people. A procession of packhorses, wagons and carts would be followed by courtiers on horseback and then the sovereign. Elizabeth I also journeyed regularly around England on a 'royal progress'. She and her court would stay in the houses of her nobles, who despite the honour of such a visit, often dreaded it due to the vast expense involved. They would be expected to entertain on a grand scale and provide gifts. Elizabeth relished such travels as they helped to boost her popularity.

PREPARING FOR A ROYAL VISIT

Explain to the children that the court of Queen Elizabeth I is to visit the great Tudor house where they work. The household must make preparations for the visit.

Invitations must be designed and made for sending to the other local gentry. Ask the children to design the family's coat of arms and motto for the front of the invitation.

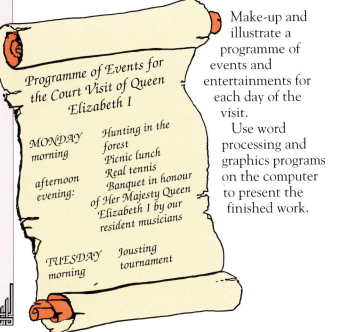

Make-up and illustrate a programme of events and entertainments for each day of the visit. Use word processing and graphics programs on the computer to present the finished work.

TUDOR DANCE

Teach the children some of the Tudor dances which would be performed during a court visit. These might include the pavane, the galliard, the almain or the La Volta. Alison and Michael Bagenal's book *Music From the Past – Tudor England* is an excellent resource for this activity, providing simple steps and music for various dances.

A FEAST FIT FOR A KING

See page 64 This is part of a 'bill of fare' from Hoghton Tower, the home of Sir Richard Hoghton whom King James I visited in August, 1617 as part of the royal progress. Discuss with the children the layout and spelling on the 'bill of fare'.

Design an activity sheet to use with the resource.

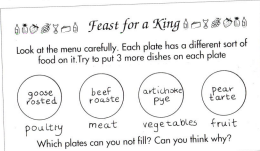

ASKING QUESTIONS

Can they interpret what was on the menu for each course of the meal?

Why are there so few vegetables on the menu?

Where would the different varieties of meat come from?

What drinks would be served with the meal – ale, wine, cider, perry not tea or coffee?

Compare this 'bill of fare' with a menu for dinner in a hotel today. What is the same? What is different?

A Stuart Menu

Place _____

Date _____ Day _____

Write the Stuart name for these

boiled chicken _____   turkey pie _____

roast lamb _____   custard _____

cold rabbit _____   pear tart _____

What do we call these dishes today?

pease buttered _____   goose rosted _____

minct pye hote _____   gamons of bacon _____

THE BREAK WITH ROME

BACKGROUND INFORMATION

When Henry VIII ascended the throne in 1509, England was a Catholic country, the king and people acknowledging the Pope in Rome as Head of the Church. When Edward VI was crowned king, nearly 40 years later, England had broken away from the Catholic Church and a new church, the Church of England, had been established.

It was the second of Henry VIII's six marriages which led to the break with Rome. Henry was desperate to have a male heir. He wished to continue the Tudor dynasty and believed that only a son would maintain the strength and prosperity of the country.

His first marriage, to Catherine of Aragon, had produced a daughter, Mary. Henry wanted to divorce Catherine and marry someone younger, a courtier named Anne Boleyn, whom he hoped might bear him a son. Divorce could only take place with the approval of the Pope. The Pope refused Henry's petition and they quarrelled. Henry decided to break away from Rome and the Catholic Church and make himself head of a new church, called the Church of England. Parliament sanctioned the split with Rome and Henry's divorce from Catherine. The king married Anne. Ironically, it was not Anne but Henry's next wife, Jane Seymour, who gave birth to his only son, Edward. Although all three of Henry's surviving children were crowned sovereign, it was his younger daughter, Elizabeth, who was to reign the longest and be the most popular of these three monarchs.

The break with Rome should be seen in the context of the religious changes which were taking place in Europe at the same time. In countries such as Switzerland, France and Germany movements to reform the Roman Catholic Church were emerging, led by men such as Zwingli, Calvin and Luther. Together with their supporters, they were protesting against the Catholic Church and, in particular, against the amount of power and authority the Pope and priests had. They wanted to change the practices and doctrines of the church.

The protestors formed various churches which were separate from Rome and known as the Protestant churches. Through Henry VIII's actions the new Church of England became one such Protestant church. There were already supporters of Protestantism in England at the time of the break with Rome and they welcomed the establishment of the new church.

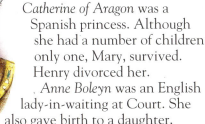

THE SIX WIVES OF HENRY VIII

Catherine of Aragon was a Spanish princess. Although she had a number of children only one, Mary, survived. Henry divorced her.

Anne Boleyn was an English lady-in-waiting at Court. She also gave birth to a daughter, Elizabeth. Henry grew tired of Anne and had her executed in 1536.

Jane Seymour, also a courtier, was the daughter of an English noble. She was reputedly Henry's favourite wife. She bore him a son, Edward, but died a few days after his birth.

Anne of Cleves was the daughter of a German duke. Henry married her for political reasons and because she was a Protestant. However, he found her unattractive and dull and they did not get on. He soon divorced her. They had no children.

Catherine Howard was the daughter of an English duke. She was almost 30 years younger than Henry. She was put on trial and executed after Henry discovered she had been unfaithful. She, too, had no children.

Catherine Parr was a Protestant English widow who looked after Henry during his last four, illness-ridden years. They had no children and she survived him.

BORN TO BE KING OR QUEEN?

England had not had a female monarch since the disputed reign of Matilda in the 12th century.

Divide the children into two mixed-gender groups Ask them to imagine they are courtiers in Henry's palace. Henry is courting Anne Boleyn. Ask one group to list all the reasons why a son would make a good heir to the throne. Ask the other group to list all the reasons why a daughter could also be a suitable heir to the throne.

It is important to discuss this issue in the context of the time and bearing in mind the views which were common then of male and female qualities. (Primogeniture in the male line is still the basis of present royal and peer succession. This could also be a subject for discussion with the children.)

*Two he divorced, two he beheaded
One was to die and one survived.*

Children are fascinated by the number of Henry VIII's wives and their fates.

Compose a rhyme or mnemonic to help them to remember the names and order of marriage of the six wives.

Use the background information and the gravestones to make a set of information cards for each wife. Include name, position in the order of wives, nationality, occupation, age when married, number and names of children, length of time married, how the marriage ended and age at death.

Write an account of each marriage from the wife's point of view.

Who's who The information could be made into an illustrated Who's Who for Henry's wives.

Use a database Information about Henry's wives could be analysed and compared.

Roundheads and Cavaliers

Teacher's notes. *Mask these notes before photocopying this sheet for the children.*
- Discuss how much protection each outfit would provide for the soldier who wore it.
- Why do soldiers today wear outfits with less protection than in the past?
- How are the outfits the same?
- How are they different?
- Put the soldiers into chronological order.

CIVIL WAR AND RESTORATION

BACKGROUND INFORMATION

Charles I, like his father James I, believed in the divine right of kings: that he was chosen by God to be king and that everyone, including Parliament, had to obey him in all matters. Charles and his Parliament could not agree about many things but especially about money. In 1629 Charles dissolved Parliament and ruled without it for 11 years.

The quarrels between king and Parliament led to the bitter Civil War. Charles gathered his supporters, known as Royalists and Cavaliers, and raised an army. Parliament also assembled an army. Their supporters, mainly Puritans, were known as Roundheads because of the way they wore their hair. The Civil War divided the country and many families, too. Often brother fought brother and father fought son.

After its army had suffered several defeats, Parliament put Oliver Cromwell in charge. He created the New Model Army, or Ironsides, who were better trained, disciplined and equipped than before. The first phase of the war lasted from 1642 to 1646. The Royalists were decisively defeated at Naseby (1645) and Charles was captured at Newark (1646) by the Scots. He escaped and the war began its final phase. Royalist risings in Wales, Essex and Kent were defeated, and a Royalist Scottish force was defeated at the battle of Preston, in 1648. Charles I was captured and put on trial. He was sentenced to death as a traitor and beheaded outside Whitehall Palace (1649).

After Charles I's death, England spent 11 years as a republic under the rule of the Lord Protector, Oliver Cromwell. Daily life was governed by the strict rules of the Puritans. All evidence of Catholicism, such as paintings, statues, crosses, altars and stained glass were removed from churches. The Puritans lived simply, wearing plain clothes. All forms of entertainment were forbidden. No one was allowed to work or play games on a Sunday. Theatres and inns were closed. Laws were passed against dancing, music, card playing, bear baiting and football.

Many people hated these harsh laws and longed for a return to life with a monarch. When Cromwell died the eldest son of Charles I was invited to return from exile abroad to become king. Charles II returned to London in triumph and the crown was 'restored'. Charles's court was lively and extravagant and the new king earned the title of 'The Merry Monarch' as he enjoyed dancing, music and horse racing and encouraged the theatre, the arts and science.

Divide the children into two groups – one supporting the Roundheads, the other the Cavaliers. Ask them to imagine they have just heard that the Battle of Naseby is over. The Roundheads have been victorious.

They must write a letter with the news to a fellow supporter. They should include a description of what their soldiers wore, why and how they fought and the outcome of the battle. Explain to the children that their reports will differ depending on their loyalties.

When England became a republic called the Commonwealth, daily life was influenced by the Puritans. Ask the children to design a poster, to be hung up on their village green, banning entertainments and giving a list of banned activities.

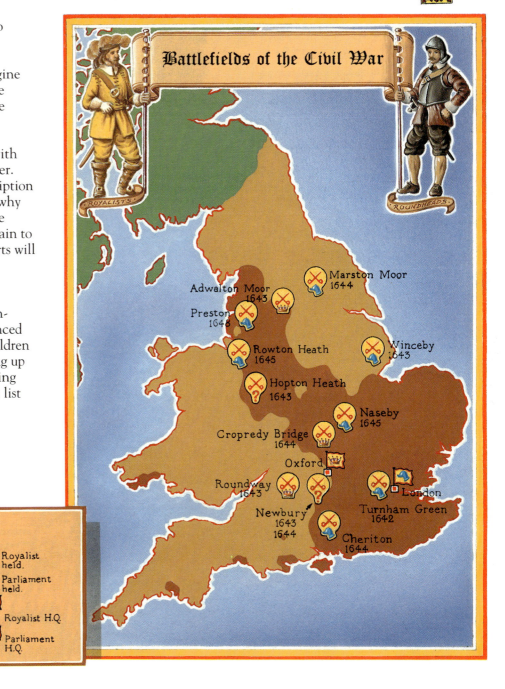

The Death Warrant of King Charles I

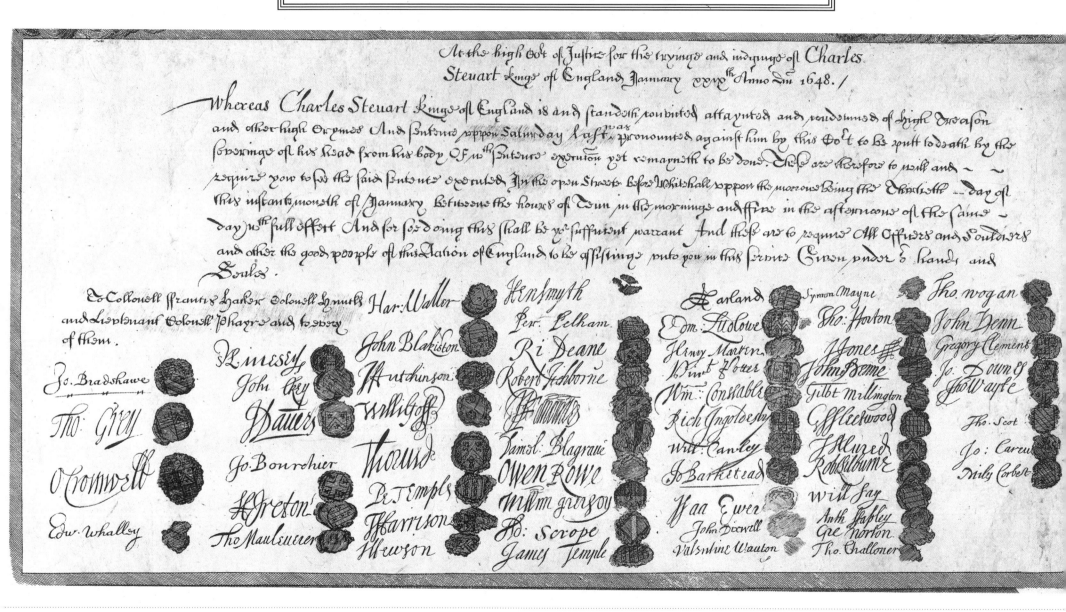

Teacher's notes. *Mask these notes before photocopying this sheet for the children.*
- Explain to the children what a death warrant is. Help them to read what is on the document.
- What was the king charged with?
- How was he put to death?
- When was he put to death?
- How many people signed the death warrant?
- What is the purpose of the seal next to each signature?
- Can the children find the name of Oliver Cromwell?

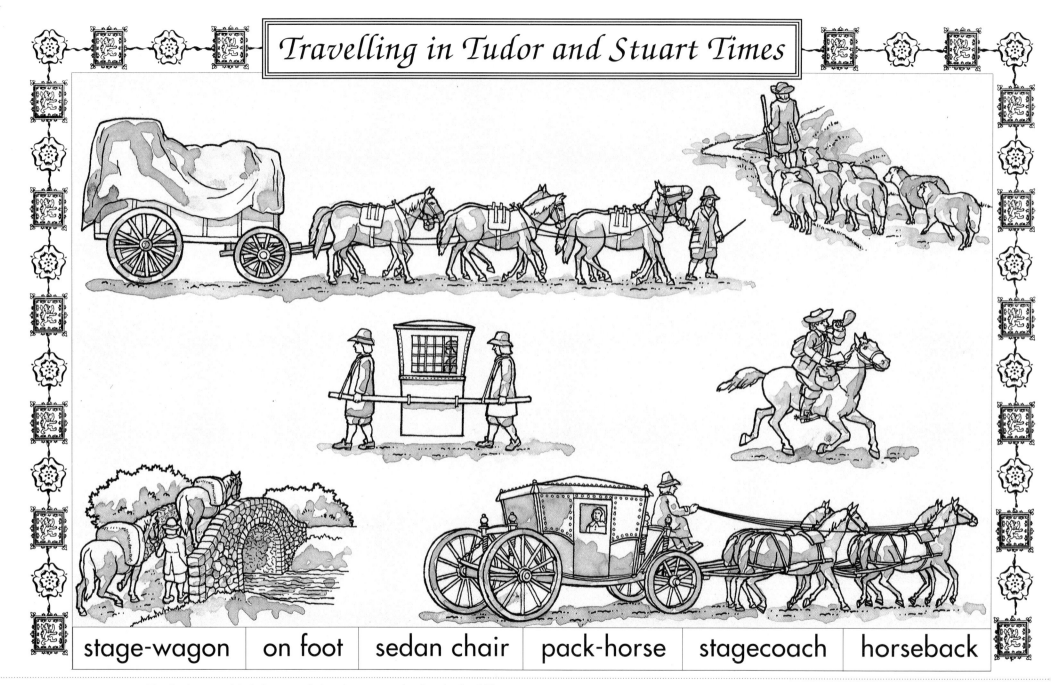

Travelling in Tudor and Stuart Times

| stage-wagon | on foot | sedan chair | pack-horse | stagecoach | horseback |

Teacher's notes. *Mask these notes before photocopying this sheet for the children.*
- It may help to enlarge this sheet on a photocopier.
- The children should cut out the pictures and labels, match and paste them.
- Use the evidence to decide what kind of people travelled in the various ways (rich/poor, boy/merchant ...).
- Can the children suggest today's equivalent to each picture?
- The children could work in pairs to research one aspect of travel. The results could contribute to a class display.

Towns, Trade and Transport 73

BACKGROUND INFORMATION

TRADE AND TOWNS

Towns were busy, noisy places crowded with people and animals. There would be traffic jams as wagons and other vehicles jostled for space in the narrow streets, with people arguing and fighting and traders shouting about their wares.

Merchants and craftsmen, such as tailors, armourers and saddlers, had apprentices – boys who were learning a trade or craft – working for them. One of their jobs was to stand in the street outside the shops touting for trade. Other goods would be bought from hawkers who strolled around the streets. Eggs, fruit, flowers, sausages, old clothes and many other items were sold from a basket or a tray hung around the hawker's neck. Wandering tradesmen, such as chimney sweeps, tinkers, ratcatchers and water carriers, called out offering their services.

At night, towns were dark, unsafe places, with only a few candle lanterns lighting the streets. When rich people ventured out at night, they would hire a 'link boy' with a torch to walk with them, for fear of thieves lurking in alleys. There was no policeforce, only watchmen, who patrolled the streets at night carrying a staff and lantern.

TRAVELLING BY ROAD

Roads were usually in a state of poor repair – full of ruts and holes, muddy in wet weather and dusty in dry weather. Highwaymen held up travellers, demanding 'Your money or your life'.

Most people travelled by foot or on horseback, or used mules or donkeys. Goods were moved around by carts, wagons or pack-horses. During the 16th century, stage-wagons began to run regular goods and passenger services between the larger towns. A stage-wagon was a large, unsprung cart with wide wheels, pulled by a team of up to ten horses. It had no seats, so the passengers sat on the floor among the goods. Typically, a journey of 100 miles would take three days. Only poorer people travelled by stage-wagon.

Coaches were introduced into Britain in the latter part of the 16th century. Only the rich could afford to own or hire them. Stagecoaches probably started about 1650, and initially ran only from London to a few large towns and only on certain days. About every 15 miles, a coach would stop at an inn (or stage) to change the tired horses and drop or pick up passengers. On journeys taking several days, the passengers would spend the nights in roadside inns.

By the mid-1600s, hackney coaches were running in London. They were for hire at a shilling a mile – too costly for most people, but popular with richer people whose fine clothes would be spoiled if they walked the filthy streets. The sedan chair was also popular at this time because of the ease with which narrow streets could be negotiated. There were private chairs as well as chairs for hire.

The Royal Mail was started by Charles I, who introduced postboys to ride the main routes delivering mail. Previously, mostly wagoners carried letters and parcels (and messages for people who could not write), although there were always couriers available.

LOOKING AT SIGNS AND SYMBOLS

Some of today's hotels and pubs originated in Tudor and Stuart times as coaching inns. The stagecoach would drive through the large archway in the centre of the inn, into a courtyard where the passengers would alight and the horses would be changed.

The children can design and make a name sign for a coaching inn. Topical names such as 'The Coach and Horses', 'The King's Head' or 'The Highwayman' could be chosen.

Can the children find any local pub or hotel signs which have Tudor or Stuart connections? Is there evidence that any local pubs or hotels were once coaching inns?

Many Tudor and Stuart shopkeepers had signs with symbols hanging outside their shops to show what they sold.

Can the children create signs for some of the shops, such as a baker, a pot seller or a wool merchant?

Are there now any shops which use signs rather than words?

Ask the children why they think written notices were not used? Provide them with symbols and ask them to deduce what the shops would have sold.

Street hawkers each had their own chants or rhymes that advertised their goods.

The children can make up a set of phrases to be shouted by traders offering goods or services. They could practise shouting them. Who can be heard above a crowd?

Are any goods and services now advertised by songs or chants? Listen to television and radio advertisements.

Living through the Plague

 Teacher's notes. *Mask these notes before photocopying this sheet for the children.*
- Ask the children to mark evidence of what caused the plague: overcrowded houses, narrow streets, rubbish, rats.
- Can they indicate the effects of the disease spreading so quickly – closed up houses, the collector of the dead, signs on the door, the watchman?
- Compare the visit of the plague doctor to that of a GP today. What happens nowadays when someone is seriously ill?
- Obtain extracts from Pepys's Diary. Compare this visual evidence to his written evidence.

THE GREAT PLAGUE 75

BACKGROUND INFORMATION

The Great Plague struck London in 1665. It was a direct consequence of the appalling conditions in which most people lived in towns at this time.

Ever since the Black Death of 1348, there had been outbreaks of bubonic plague in towns, but never before had there been such a severe and prolonged epidemic. In the stifling heat of the summer of 1665, the plague – for which there was no known cure – struck London with such force that the death toll was to reach over 3000 a week.

The disease spread rapidly among the large families who lived in overcrowded, dirty houses without fresh water or proper sanitation. The dark, narrow, squalid streets where rubbish was piled up outside houses and where sewage ran freely over the cobbles, provided an excellent breeding ground for rats, on which lived the fleas that carried the plague.

Londoners put forward their own theories as to the causes of the plague. Some people believed that it was carried in the air and lit blazing bonfires to burn it out. Others believed that the plague was a disease in the ground, or that it was sent by God to punish people for their sins, or that it was deliberately spread by evil people.

The disease was painful, quick acting and usually fatal. A home where a plague victim lived had a red cross painted on the door, often accompanied by the words 'Lord have mercy on us'. The house would be closed up, food left outside and a watchman posted to stop people entering or leaving. Doctors who risked visiting such homes wore hooded outfits with beaks which were stuffed with herbs in the hope that they would filter and clean the air.

As the plague took hold, there were too many victims to bury decently. Corpses were collected by men with carts who toured the streets at night, tolling a bell and shouting 'Bring out your dead'. The bodies were dumped in deep 'plague pits' outside the city. People left for the country to avoid the plague but they often took the disease with them. It was not until the end of the year when the frosts set in that the plague died out.

*Ring a ring of roses,
A pocket full of posies,
Atishoo, atishoo,
We all fall down*

The nursery rhyme 'Ring-a-ring of roses' originates from the time of the Great Plague. Through use of the rhyme explain to the children that the ring of roses depicts the red, purple and black blotches appearing on the victim's skin, which identified the plague. Posies were the nosegays used to cover the smell of the plague and the atishoo was the sneeze which was a symptom of the disease

The children could make their own scented pomanders using oranges and cloves, and collect or make pot-pourri for the classroom.

USING PEPYS'S DIARY

Introduce the children to Samuel Pepys, who worked in the Navy Office. He kept a diary in a special form of shorthand which detailed events at the time. His shorthand formed a secret code which other people, especially his wife, could not read and which enabled him to write at speed.

Pepys's Diary contains excellent primary source evidence for the Great Plague and the Fire of London (see pages 76-77).

Use, for example, extracts such as this one for 18 July 1665: *'I was much troubled …to hear …how the officers do bury the dead in the open.'* Ask the children to imagine they live in a house in which someone has the plague. Their own diary can describe what happens to the victim and the family. How do they get food? Why is there a watchman outside? How do they feel? Who will be next?

MAKE A 17TH CENTURY POMANDER

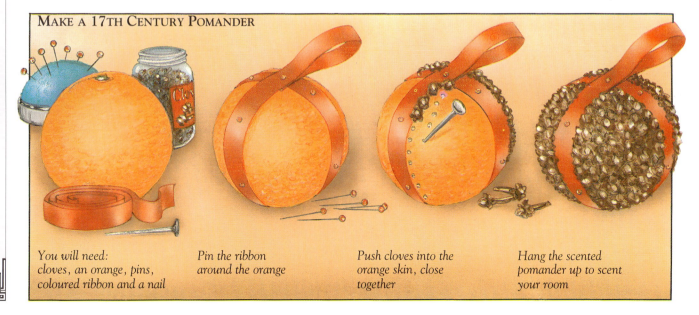

You will need: cloves, an orange, pins, coloured ribbon and a nail

Pin the ribbon around the orange

Push cloves into the orange skin, close together

Hang the scented pomander up to scent your room

Extracts from Samuel Pepys's Diary

Samuel Pepys wrote in his diary in a secret shorthand. The extract on the left reads as follows:

2 September 1666: Jane called us up about three in the morning, to tell us of a great fire they saw in the City. So I rose...and went to her window...I thought it far enough off; and so went to bed again...

2 September 1666: About seven rose again...Jane comes and tells me that she hears that above 300 houses have been burned down tonight by the fire we saw...and that it is now burning by London Bridge.

2 September 1666: Everybody endeavouring to remove their goods, and flinging them into the river or bringing them into lighters...poor people staying in their houses as long as till the very fire touched them.

2 September 1666: Having...seen the fire rage every way, and nobody to my sight, endeavouring to quench it, but to...leave all to the fire...and the wind mighty high and driving it into the City: and everything, after so long a drought, proving combustible...

2 September 1666: ...to Whitehall...and the King commanded me to go to my Lord Mayor from him, and command him to spare no houses, but to pull down before the fire every way.

2 September 1666: ...saw the fire grow; and, as it grew darker, appeared more and more, and in corners and upon steeples, and between churches and houses, as far as we could see...

3 September 1666: About four o'clock in the morning, my Lady Batten sent me a cart to carry away all my money, and plate, and best things...which I did, riding myself in my nightgown in the cart...

4 September 1666: Sir W. Pen and I did dig another, (pit in the garden) and put our wine in it; and I my Parmazan cheese...and some other things.

4 September 1666: Now begins the practice of blowing up of houses in Tower Street...which at first did frighten people...but it stopped the fire where it was done... .

7 September 1666: Up by five o'clock; and blessed be God! find all well...

Teacher's notes. *Mask these notes before photocopying this sheet for the children.*
- These extracts could be enlarged on the photocopier, mounted on card and then laminated. The children could then work with a variable number of extracts at the teacher's discretion.
- Ask the children to identify evidence of when the fire started; how and why it spread; attempts to put it out; what Pepys thought was worth saving; the difference between rich and poor when the fire was extinguished.
- Mix up the extracts and ask the children to sequence them chronologically.
- Compare this written evidence with visual evidence.

London's Burning 77

Background Information

A year after the plague struck London, the city was devastated by the Great Fire. This was another tragedy helped by the building methods and living conditions of the times.

The Great Fire started accidentally in the early hours of Sunday, 2 September 1666, in a baker's shop in Pudding Lane, close to London Bridge. The summer had been hot and dry – everything was so much tinder. The fire spread quickly through the narrow streets of cramped, overhanging, timber-framed houses, the flames being driven by a strong wind. The fire-fighting equipment was crude and inadequate. Many people fought bravely to douse the flames and pull down houses in the path of the fire, but the fire swept rapidly through the city. People were terrified and, taking the belongings they could carry or load on to a cart, they made for the River Thames or the open countryside.

When the fire became a raging inferno, the king ordered that houses be blown up with gunpowder to create wide fire breaks. At last, the wind changed direction, the fire was brought under control and the city was left full of smoke and ruined buildings. More than 13 000 houses, 89 churches, including St Paul's Cathedral, and many public buildings were destroyed. Over 100 000 people were left homeless, although amazingly only a handful had died. Out of the destruction rose a city with new churches, fine buildings and safer houses built in stone or brick and set in wider, cleaner streets. The improved living conditions also did much to reduce the chances of the plague returning.

I was There

The children can imagine they are some of the various characters involved in the Great Fire. These might include:
- a member of a family whose house lay in the path of the fire debating whether to escape
- a boatman taking people across the river to safety
- a firefighter pulling houses down
- the Lord Mayor watching his city engulfed in flames.

Encourage the children to think about the fire and its effects from their own point of view. Ideas could be written down or recorded on tape.

Using Paintings

A painting is a record of an artist's impression of an event or scene at one point in time. Using paintings with children helps their understanding that different people interpret things in different ways. As artists can be selective in what they include in their work, a painting may not provide a complete record or all the evidence available.

Chronological Sequencing

Sequencing artefacts helps children to develop an understanding of chronology. They can see how things change or stay the same over time. If actual artefacts are not available, cut up and mount pictures from old books and use them for sequencing.

The children could sequence photographs of firefighting equipment.

Investigating Monuments

Monuments provide a valuable source of evidence that a person lived or an event took place.

The Monument, designed by Sir Christopher Wren, was built near Pudding Lane to commemorate the outbreak of the fire. The children could make a model of the Monument. Can they find any local monuments? Why were they erected? Were the children to erect a monument today, who or what would it commemorate? What would it be like?

Ask them to think about how the equipment would be used, the problems involved, where water would come from and how people could be rescued from a burning house.

They can identify similarities and differences between Stuart and modern apparatus.

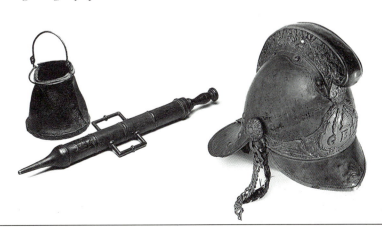

Religious Changes

Background Information

Throughout Tudor and Stuart times, people suffered for their religious beliefs, often undergoing bitter persecution and even dying for their faith. Each of the three main religious groups, although all Christian, had different kinds of church and forms of worship. The Catholics recognised the Pope in Rome as their leader. The members of the Church of England recognised the monarch as the head of their church. They were Protestants in that they 'protested' against the authority of the Pope, but retained some aspects of the Catholic liturgy. The Puritans disliked the elaborate rituals of both these churches, preferring simple services in plain buildings.

At the time of Henry VIII's reign, the Catholic monasteries were rich and had large estates. After Henry had broken with Rome and set up the Church of England, he saw the monks and nuns as a threat to his authority. He also needed an extra source of income. Using the excuse that the monasteries were run incompetently, Henry dissolved them, seizing their lands and confiscating their wealth for himself. Monastic buildings were stripped and looted. They were then abandoned and allowed to fall into ruins.

In Edward VI's reign, efforts were continued to make England a Protestant country and strengthen the Church of England. All symbols of Catholic imagery such as ornaments, shrines and stained glass windows were removed from churches. In 1549, the first English Prayer Book was introduced, having been translated from the original Latin. This was placed in every parish church alongside the English translation of the Bible which Henry VII had introduced.

When Mary I succeeded to the throne, she tried to convert England back to Catholicism. It was now the turn of the Protestants to face persecution, many of them being tortured and burnt to death at the stake.

During James I's reign, only those Protestants belonging to the Church of England were free from persecution. Catholics and Puritans were not allowed to worship freely. Attendance at church on Sunday was compulsory, a fine or even imprisonment being the penalty for not doing so. James I wanted a new translation of the Bible which everyone could understand. A group of scholars and clerics began work in 1605. In 1611, the *Authorised Version of the Bible* or *King James's Bible* was published and had to be used in every parish church.

The Dissolution of the Monastries

Convent Seale Evidence & writing to the kinge
Ornaments valued ———— £19 9s 7d
Plate 39 ounzes ———— £6 10s ———— Money nil
Corne valued, severid & unseverid £19
Cattayle valued at £17 5s   Dettes due too
the howse ———— £8 2s 6d & 4 quarts of barleye
Dettes that the howse owyth ———— £9 2s

Henry began by dissolving the smaller monastries, 318 closures bringing him £20 000. Inventories of the assets and debts of the monastries were made.

Using the evidence Some children may be able to work with the original extract, others will need to use the transcript alongside.

Translate the extract into modern English. This task can be simplified by focusing on one word at a time in chart form.

Tudor times	Today
kinge	
corne	
howse	

How much did things cost? Some children may be able to convert this to decimal currency:
12d (pence) = 1s (shilling), 20s = £1.

Item	Cost
	£ s d
Cattayle	17 5 0

Discussion should focus on what £1 would buy then and now.

Show the children the title page of the *Authorised Version of the Bible*. Who authorised this translation? Where is the evidence? Where should this Bible be read?

Compare the title page with that from a modern bible such as the *Good News Bible* or the *New English Bible*.

Read the children these extracts from the *King James's Bible* and the *New English Bible*.

What similarities and differences can the children find?

Authorised Version
And when Jesus was entered into Capernaum, there came unto him a centurion, beseeching him and saying, Lord, my servant lieth at home sick of the palsy, grievously tormented. And Jesus saith unto him, I will come and heal him.
Matthew, Ch 8, v 5-7

New English Bible
When he had entered Capernaum a centurion came up to ask his help. 'Sir', he said, 'a boy of mine lies sick at home, paralysed and racked with pain.' Jesus said, 'I will come and cure him.'
Matthew, Ch 8, v 5-7

James I and Religion

79

Background Information

During James I's reign there were many Catholics who remained loyal to the Pope and their faith. They had to worship secretly. Catholic priests travelled in disguise from house to house or lived in secret in the homes of rich families. The king's men regularly searched for such priests, who lived with the constant fear that they could be imprisoned or put to death if discovered. This fear led to the building of hiding places, called 'priest holes', in many Catholic houses. These hideaways could be in a chimney, beneath a fireplace, behind oak panelling or in hollowed out stone walls. The holes were invariably dark, cold and had little ventilation. When in danger of being discovered, the priest, his vestments and all the trappings of a Catholic mass could be hidden in the secret place. Sometimes priests had to remain hidden for days at a time.

The Gunpowder Plot

James I's treatment of the Catholics led to several plots against him, the most famous being the Gunpowder Plot of 1605. Under the leadership of Robert Catesby and Thomas Percy, a group of Catholic noblemen conspired to execute a daring crime. They planned to blow up the Houses of Parliament and the king during the state opening of Parliament. The plotters had smuggled in and hidden 36 barrels of gunpowder behind a pile of wood in a cellar under the House of Lords. One of the conspirators, worried about the safety of some friends who would be in Parliament at the time of the planned explosion, wrote a warning letter to one of them. This warning was passed on and the buildings were searched by the king's men. One of the plotters, Guy Fawkes, who was an expert in the use of explosives, was found guarding the barrels of gunpowder. He was arrested and tortured but refused to reveal the names of his accomplices. The other conspirators tried to escape – some were shot, the rest were captured and hung, drawn and quartered.

The story of Guy Fawkes is in Time and Place *Flip-over Book 3*. Read the story. The children may recall elements. Stress the need to investigate how we know. What evidence do we have?

The Search for a Priest

Before newspapers were published regularly in the early 1700s, people learnt about news from broadsheets or pamphlets, which often took the form of a series of illustrations.

Using this photograph of a priest hole as a stimulus, ask the children to create a sequence of illustrations based on the search for a priest in the house of a rich Catholic family.

This could include the family receiving bread from the priest; a servant rushing in to warn that the king's men are on their way; helping the priest to hide in the priest hole; the arrival of the king's men and their search of the house.

This activity could also be developed into some work in drama.

Investigating Ceremonies

Many events in the past are celebrated or remembered by ceremonies or rituals. These may have direct links with the historical event or symbolise it in some way. Ask the children to list traditions, ceremonies or celebrations which are linked to the past.

Special days	Event remembered
Christmas	Birth of Jesus
Holi	Spring
Remembrance Day	World War 1

Talk to the children about the rituals associated with the Gunpowder Plot. By tradition, bonfires are lit on 5 November, the day after the plot was discovered, and a figure of Guy Fawkes is often burnt on top of a fire. Lighting fireworks symbolises the explosives hidden by the conspirators. Today, there is still a ritual search of the cellars in the Houses of Parliament by the Yeoman of the Guard before Parliament is opened by the sovereign.

The Plot

Use page 80 to introduce the children to the Gunpowder Plotters.

Ask the children to imagine they are on-the-spot reporters at the time when the king's men break into the cellars under the House of Lords and find Guy Fawkes about to light the fuse to the gunpowder.

They must produce a report describing the scene and interviews with the people involved. Talk to the children about how they could get the background to the story. Would people's comments be accurate facts or merely opinions?

The report could be used in a computer program such as Front Page Extra or recorded on tape.

Treason and Plot

Guido Fawkes

Guido

Teacher's notes. *Mask these notes before photocopying this sheet for the children.*
These three pieces of evidence can be used separately or together.
- **The plotters** From this picture, the children can identify the name of the conspirators. How can we tell whether these were poor people or 'gentlemen'? Were any related? Identify the man we call Guy Fawkes. What was he known as then?
- **Guy Fawkes' lantern** Why would Guy Fawkes have needed a lantern? How does it compare with a modern torch? What is the source of light? What risk did Guy Fawkes take by using such a lantern?
- **The signatures** The signatures were made before and after torture. The children should use the evidence to determine whose signatures they are, the differences between the two and probable explanations for these differences. How does the spelling of Fawkes' signature differ from the first picture and from our modern spelling?
- **Sequence the evidence** The children should tell the story of the Gunpowder Plot and illustrate it, using the evidence on this page in the correct sequence.

Exploration and Empire

Background Information

The reigns of the Tudors and Stuarts were filled with exploration and discovery. Certain sea captains of Elizabeth I's reign were nicknamed 'sea dogs'. They regularly attacked and captured Spanish treasure ships carrying home their valuable cargoes from the Spanish empire in South America.

One such privateer was Sir Francis Drake, who is probably best remembered as the first Briton to circumnavigate the world. Drake set out from Plymouth in 1577, in his ship the 'Golden Hind'. After a journey taking nearly three years (see map on right), he returned to England a hero and with a fortune in captured treasure.

Sir Francis Drake also played a leading role in the defeat of the Spanish Armada in 1588, when the plans of King Philip II of Spain to invade and conquer England were thwarted. Drake had already delayed the king's plans the previous year when, during a surprise attack, he destroyed many of the Spanish ships in Cadiz. Drake was one of the commanders of the English fleet which sailed from Plymouth to fight successfully the Spanish fleet in the English Channel.

By the end of the Stuart era, there were several English colonies along the east coast of America.

In the late 1580s, Sir Walter Raleigh, a soldier, poet and court favourite of Elizabeth's, had financed two unsuccessful attempts to found a colony on Roanoke Island. The early settlers were frustrated by problems with crops, disease, famine and the hostile, native American Indians. However, Raleigh's expeditions did claim the whole area in the Queen's name – calling it Virginia in her honour. He also brought back two plants previously unknown in Britain – tobacco and the potato. (The Spanish and Portuguese had already introduced them to continental Europe.) Raleigh's final expeditions were fruitless, he fell from grace and James I eventually had him executed, in part to placate the King of Spain. It was not until 1607 that the first successful English colony was founded at Jamestown.

In 1620 a group of Puritan families, disillusioned with life in England and Holland, crossed the Atlantic in the 'Mayflower', hoping to establish a community where they would be able to worship freely. These so-called Pilgrim Fathers landed at a place, to the north of Virginia, which they named Plymouth Rock. After much hardship, their colony prospered and grew into the area still known as New England.

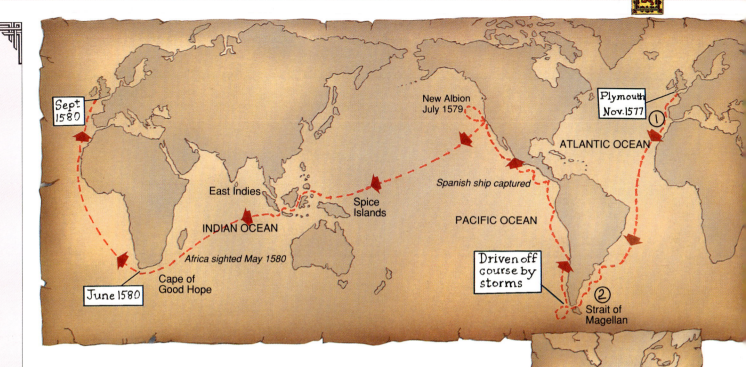

The map above shows the route taken by Sir Francis Drake on his voyage around the world between 1577 and 1580.

The children could draw in Drake's route on an enlarged world map and add the relevant place names. Each stage of his journey could be numbered and an illustration or some notes added to show what happened at each point on his voyage. For example, 'Left Plymouth, England, 1577'.

When the Spanish Armada was first sighted sailing eastwards up the English Channel, lookouts on the coast lit the first of a chain of hill-top beacons to warn people to prepare for an invasion.

Can the children make a list of the preparations people who lived in the towns on the south coast of England would have made when they heard the news about the Armada?

How would news about an important national event travel around the country today?

The Puritan settlers were known as the Pilgrim Fathers. Explain to the children what a pilgrim and a pilgrimage are. Can they work out why the first Puritan colonists were so called?

This map shows some of the early British colonies in north-east America. Ask the children to deduce for whom the colonies and the towns of Jamestown, Charleston and Raleigh were named. Some settlements took the names of British towns or villages, such as Plymouth, Washington, Richmond, Cambridge, Weymouth, Dover and Boston. Can the children find the original place names in an atlas of the British Isles? Why did the settlers choose familiar names?

Views of Women

Teacher's notes. *Mask these notes before photocopying this sheet for the children.*
These five pieces of evidence can be used separately or alongside each other. The children should be asked what the evidence tells us about women. The list of housewives' skills presents the conventional view of women. Did all women feel this way?
• 'Though you be weake ...' Jane Owen, 1634
• 'But can she spin?' King James I's response to a woman presented at court because she was regarded as accomplished.
• The Roxburghe Ballads: woodcut of haymaking. Evidence of women's work, which was often not recognised. It extended beyond household duties.
• 'There is no justification...' Mary Astell, c1690.
• *The Accomplish't Ladys Delight* by Hannah Wolley, 1675.
• This shows women making medicines, preserving, cooking and beautifying themselves.

LOCAL HISTORY

WHAT IS LOCAL HISTORY?

There is no precise definition of local history. It can relate to a village or country area; to a town or urban neighbourhood; or even to a county or group of counties. In general, though, the focus of study is likely to be the place where children live and go to school.

This does not mean, however, that all the evidence children use in studying local history must relate to their immediate surroundings. All too often, such evidence is hard to unearth. Besides, material drawn from further afield often aids children's understanding, without undermining the local emphasis of their work.

TYPES OF LOCAL HISTORY

Three types are distinguished in the National Curriculum:
- An aspect of a local community over a long period of time. Examples include education, leisure, religion and home life.
- An aspect of a local community during a short period of time or the community's involvement with a particular event. Examples include land enclosure and the impact of the World Wars.
- An aspect of a local community which illustrates developments taught in other study units. Examples include Victorian children, Roman settlement and post-war immigration.

	HISTORY														
ATTAINMENT TARGETS	1									2			3		
LEVELS	2			3			4			2	3	4	2	3	4
STATEMENTS	a	b	c	a	b	c	a	b	c	a	a	a	a	a	a
108 Timeline		•	•	•	•	•	•	•	•	•	•	•	•	•	•
110-111 Planning a local HSU		•	•	•	•	•	•	•			•		•	•	•
112 Looking at artefacts				•			•							•	•
113 Local history sources				•	•	•	•	•	•		•		•	•	•
114 Searching for clues					•	•	•	•							•
115 Oral sources				•			•				•				•
116 Written sources					•										
118-119 Schools 100 years ago		•	•	•	•	•	•	•	•		•		•	•	•
120-121 School curriculum		•	•	•	•			•	•				•		•
122-123 In the playground		•	•	•	•			•					•		•
124-125 Teaching and teachers		•	•	•	•	•					•	•	•	•	•
126-127 Scholars	•	•	•	•	•		•		•				•	•	•
128 School premises		•	•	•	•								•	•	•

Whether long-term local history study units will cover the 1000-year time span required for other long-term study units is uncertain. Some may, but much will depend on the availability of suitable source material and on the extent of the geographical area chosen. For the most part, it is probably more realistic to take a period covering a few hundred years. This should still give a sufficient time span for children to explore long-term developments in their locality.

The National Curriculum does not make any precise distinction between a short and long-period study unit in local history. Probably, however, the former will not cover more than a few decades. The impact of the First or Second World War on a locality gives especially striking examples, not only because they meet the general requirements for local history study units but also because they relate to any locality and are relatively easy to resource.

A unit of local history which links with another HSU may be taught separately, with children going from the general to the particular. In this way, a context for local work is readily established. Alternatively, local material may be incorporated within the more general material as appropriate. This enables selected aspects of the HSU to be explored in appreciable depth.

LOCAL HISTORY STUDY UNIT: PLANNING SHEET

Theme _____

Age group _____

Available sources	Location	Adaptation needed (if any)

Key questions	Teaching approach	Attainment targets

PLANNING A LOCAL HISTORY STUDY UNIT

This chart raises key issues that need to be addressed if local history study units are to be effectively planned and taught. These issues are considered in detail throughout the chapter.

Are adequate sources available to teach the theme?
As a rule, local source material will be available in most localities for themes relating to 19th and 20th century developments. For earlier periods, the position is more variable. Clearly, this will have a strong bearing on the choice of themes for local history study units.

What are the key questions children might ask?
Within any theme that is selected, it will be necessary to encourage the children to raise questions which they will investigate. Each question will form the basis of one or more lessons and may well draw on different types of source material.

Where are the teaching resources located?
Amongst local organisations that are able to provide teaching resources, reference libraries and museums are likely to prove especially helpful. Additionally, studying the local built environment can often provide important historical insights, whilst oral evidence can be generated by the children themselves.

What are the most appropriate themes to choose?
There are many possibilities, among which those dealing with children in the past are likely to have particular appeal. But children will also be interested in the way local communities as a whole lived in the past and in how these communities were affected by national and international events. Major wars and changing leisure patterns provide examples.

Is the theme suitable for the age range?
For younger juniors especially, local history units based on charting the growth of local communities may prove rather complex and abstract. Narrowing down to a particular theme will provide a clear focus and will allow issues to be examined in some depth.

Will the sources need adapting for classroom use?
This is a particularly important issue with regard to young children, since there is little point in presenting them with primary source material they are unable to read. Careful selection of material is necessary, therefore, perhaps accompanied by transcription and editing.

Does the plan meet National Curriculum requirements?
Apart from devising different types of local history unit, it is necessary to ensure that an important historical issue is being investigated and that local developments are related to national ones. With regard to the former, a key point is to give the unit a broad enough focus. Thus, the history of an individual school or church will provide far fewer insights into the development of a community than will a more general study of its educational or religious history. As to the latter, the essential point is to provide a context for local history. Without this, children will have difficulty in appreciating the significance of their findings and in explaining them.

What will be the teaching approach?
Thought should be given to the balance between group and class teaching. The former makes more economical use of teaching resources, though the latter may be preferred at the outset and in drawing out the main conclusions.

LOCAL HISTORY STUDY UNIT: PLANNING SHEET

Theme: Local schools in early 1900s   Age group: Year 4.

Available sources	Location	Adaptation needed (if any)
Oral testimony	Relatives and friends	Check all responses for legibility (tapes) Maybe edit
Logbook extracts	Records office	Transcribe and edit
Attendance register	Records office	Photocopy 3 or 4 pages
Visual sources	Library archives	" " "
Photos of old schools	Library archives	" " "
Instruction manual	Reference library	Photocopy extracts
Pupils' copy books	Records office	Photocopy 2 pages
Autobiographies	Library/bookshop	Brief extract/edit if required
Old school plans	Records office	Photocopy and enlarge

Key questions	Teaching approach	Attainment targets
What is oral history?	Read to children autobiographical extracts. Discuss why oral testimony is valuable and how we get it.	AT 1 L2b, 3a,b,c, 4,a,b AT 2 L2, L3, L4. AT 3 L2,L3 AT 1 L.2 b, C, 3c 4a, AT3 L.2,3.
What were the lessons like? What did children do at playtime?	Role play/stimulation. Teach a Victorian lesson 'The Baker' from instruction manual. In pairs: photograph interpretation of drill lesson Whole class: drill lesson in yard Design questions for visitor (70 years old) Compare now/1930s/1900s.	AT 1 L.2b,c L.3C, L4a AT 3 L.2, L.3. AT 1 L.2b,c, 3a,b,c, L4a AT 2 L.3 AT 3 L.2, L.3; L.4.

Looking at Artefacts

Draw the artefact

Draw a modern artefact which does the same job

What is it made from? ....

Is it damaged or mended? ....

How? ....

Does it have parts that move? ....

Do you think anything is missing from it? ....

If so, what? ....

Has it been used a lot? ....

How can you tell? ....

Is it old or new? ....

How can you tell? ....

Did it have a use? ....

If so, what was it? ....

Does it remind you of anything you have seen before? ....

If so, what? ....

Do we use objects like this today? ....

What is it? ....

Who would have used it? ....

Teacher's notes. *Mask these notes before photocopying this sheet for the children.*
- The children should have the opportunity to investigate artefacts at first hand.
- The two left-hand boxes could be enlarged on a photocopier.
- The questions may be provided orally, a few at a time, to focus observation and discussion.

LOCAL HISTORY SOURCES   113

Local history sources may be grouped into the four types framed below. There is some overlap between the types – maps, for example, being both a written and a visual source. For the most part, however, the categories hold true and provide a useful aid in planning HSUs.

Local history sources

Source	Example
Written: by hand / printed	School log-books / Newspaper extracts
Visual	Photographs
Oral testimony	Taped conversation
Physical: artefacts / landscape features	Household utensils / Houses

ARTEFACTS

Artefacts (objects made by people) include a wide range of items that past generations have left. They can be particularly helpful in teaching such historical themes as 'Schools' and 'Home life', and are ideal for helping children to ask questions about the past. Handling artefacts or even studying photographs of them enables children to work out a great deal about how people in the past lived.

AT 2: Interpretations of history
Level 2
Invite two adults to describe their experiences with pens and inkwells. One should have had success, the other difficulty.

Level 3
In a statement such as 'Using a pen and ink often led to blotting but the writing produced was beautiful', can the children distinguish between fact and point of view?

AT 3: The use of historical sources
Level 2
Use the artefacts to help the children to recognise how school children wrote in the past.

Level 3
Deduce from the blotting paper that the old style pen was capable of making more mess than a modern pen.

Level 4
Examine the artefacts alongside other historical sources, such as exercise books written at the time when the pens were used.

AT 1: Knowledge and understanding of history
Level 2
(a) Provide the children with a fountain pen and a Biro in addition to the artefact. Ask the children to place them in chronological order.
(b) Based on their experience of writing with pen and ink, ask the children why people in the past used blotting paper.
(c) Compare whatever the children use today with the pen and ink set.

Level 3
(a) Illustrate, by introducing a slate pencil or a word processor, how change has occurred over the past 100 years.
(b) Discuss how the development of the Biro removed the need for ink wells.
(c) Compare the classroom of 20 years ago (fountain pen) with that of 100 years ago (slate pencil).

Level 4
(a) Recognise that writing on paper is a continuing feature of classroom practice but that the instrument used has changed.
(b) Raise awareness that in addition to inventions (the Biro, for example) wealth has also influenced change.
(c) Be aware that the pen and inkwell are only one feature among many which typify schooling at a particular time (consider seating, display, curriculum and punishment).

Many sources can generate questions and activities related to all three ATs.

114 SEARCHING FOR CLUES

LANDSCAPE FEATURES
These include buildings and transport, which can provide evidence of great value in meeting the requirements of AT 1 and AT 3.

Where children can undertake fieldwork, landscape evidence can be used directly. If this is difficult, it may be necessary to take photographs of particular landscape features for classroom use.

COMPARE AND CONTRAST
Children can describe key features of housing in the school locality and then make comparisons with housing further afield, perhaps of earlier or later date.

Number of windows
Reveals number of rooms, unless any rooms had more than one window.

Fanlight above door
Indicates an inner hallway, which gave privacy in the front room (parlour).

Number of chimney pots
Shows how many rooms had fireplaces and could therefore be heated before electricity and/or gas were installed.

Height of house
For health reasons, by-laws stipulated minimum heights for rooms in mid and late-Victorian houses. Hence they are tall. Counting courses of bricks gives the height of outer walls.

Size of windows
With high rooms, tall windows could be fitted to facilitate good natural lighting

Comparing houses

Observation	Victorian	Modern
Is there a chimney?	Yes	Yes
If so, how many pots?	Three	One
Is there a driveway?	No	Yes
Is the house part of a row?	Yes	No
Draw the window shape.		
Is there a fanlight above the front door?	Yes	No
Is there a front garden?	No	Yes
Draw the brick bonding.		

Brick bonds
Three common types are found:

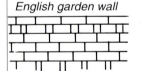
English garden wall

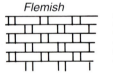
Flemish

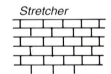
Stretcher

Modern houses have cavity walls to prevent damp from penetrating. Where header courses are found, as is usual in Victorian terraces, the bricks usually go through the wall from front to back. Thus, there is no cavity.

VISUAL SOURCES
Contemporaneous photographs are perhaps the most obvious visual source for local history. However, a great deal can also be discovered about local people in the past, and about the environment in which they lived, from contemporaneous paintings, drawings and engravings. They constitute important sources with regard to activities in AT 1, strand C (differences) and AT 3 (sources).

As with physical sources, children will need to gain experience in asking questions of visual sources, looking at the type of scene shown, what people are doing and wearing, what time period is depicted, and so on.

As a rule, contemporaneous visual sources will be more plentiful for urban than for rural localities. Accordingly, village studies might be extended to embrace a local town, perhaps to consider differences in the way that town and country dwellers led their lives.

Oral Sources

The Importance of Oral Testimony

A major advantage of using oral testimony in local history teaching is that it often provides insights which are not available from any other source. It can also be very real and immediate to young children, especially if it is derived from people they know. Oral testimony can be used in meeting all the Attainment Targets in history but has particular value with regard to AT 2: Interpretations of history.

On the other hand, oral testimony is largely confined to the 20th century. Moreover, it may provide evidence which is highly individualistic and which does not represent the experiences or attitudes of local people in general.

Oral testimony can be recorded in writing or on tape.

Taped Extracts

Audio or video cassettes can be used. Whichever is chosen, the extract should be short and clear, if necessary edited by the teacher, and accompanied by a focused task for the children. Otherwise, there is the likelihood of the children becoming restless.

Focused Task

Use oral evidence to help children distinguish between a fact and a point of view (AT 2, Level 3).

School in 1957	
Fact	Point of view
Most people had a school dinner	The dinners were awful

This activity is best done in small groups rather than the whole class listening to a series of tapes.

Visitors to the Classroom

The children should appreciate that recollections of the same events may vary. The best way to develop this understanding is to start with members of the class talking about their own recollections of Reception Class. Are their descriptions the same?

The children should also understand that everyone has a history. So it is important to invite visitors of different ages to share their past experiences.

Try to support oral testimony with other evidence of the past. For example, people in their teens, 20s, 30s ...

A visitor could be recorded on audio tape or video by the children, but it is important to check beforehand that this is acceptable to the guest.

Visiting the Elderly

The children can gain a great deal from this. However, unless properly structured, there is a danger of rambling responses from some interviewees.

Preparing Questionnaires

This will help to ensure that all the respondents address the same issues, so that the children will be better placed to attempt generalisations from the evidence they glean. Examples of questions are given below.

Questions on school life

In the classroom
1 Can you describe your classroom?
2 How was it heated?
3 Did it have high windows?
4 Can you describe the desks or tables you sat at?

Lessons
5 What subjects were you taught?
*6 Which was your favourite lesson and why?
*7 Which lesson or lessons did you not like and why?
8 Did you have any special lessons?
9 What did you write with?

Pupils
10 What clothes and footwear did you have for school?
11 How old were you when you started school? What year was that?
12 How old were you when you finished school?
13 What times did your school day start and finish?
14 How did you get to and from school?
15 How far did you live from school?
16 What happened when you were late for school?

Teaching
17 Were you taught in a group or as a class?
*18 Do you think your teachers were strict? If so, in what ways?
19 What do you remember about the textbooks you had?
20 Can you give details of any tests you had?

Playtime and lunchtime
21 What was the playground like?
22 What did you play in the playground?
23 How long did you have for lunch?
24 Did you have school lunches? If not, what did you do for lunch?

Opinions on your school
*25 Did you enjoy or dislike it? Please say why?
*26 Do you think schools have become better or worse? Please say why?

Most questions invite a factual response, but those marked with an asterisk elicit points of view.

116 WRITTEN SOURCES

USING WRITTEN SOURCES

As with oral testimony, written sources need to be chosen with care. The prime criterion is that the children should be able either to read them or to understand them if they are read aloud by the teacher. Extracts should be brief enough to maintain interest and lend themselves to pupil activity.

HANDWRITTEN MATERIAL

Local history sources written in a contemporary hand may not be too difficult for young children to read. Much will depend on the neatness of the writing and whether most of the words used are familiar. An examination of the difference between past and present styles of writing provide a useful AT 1 activity.

PRINTED MATERIAL

Printed contemporaneous material for use in local history teaching will normally be found in books and articles, newspapers and posters, and reports and surveys.

A great deal of local evidence can be obtained from national publications, especially Parliamentary papers. These comprise several groups of records, amongst which are Parliamentary Commissions (such as the 1832 Poor Law Commission) and reports to Parliament (including census reports).

Secondary sources

Articles and books published by local historians will also be useful, not least in providing background detail. The volumes of the Victoria County Histories are a notable example. There are also books concerned with the research methods used by local historians, some of which can be adapted for classroom use.

Obtaining Source Materials

Local Reference Library
For written and visual sources, the local reference library is usually the best place to start. Often, there is a local studies section. Make an appointment to see the librarian in charge, explaining who you are and what work you are planning. Time can then be set aside for you.

Libraries frequently publish booklets giving details of their local history holdings. Facsimiles of some items in their collection may be available and photocopies, or photographic prints, can often be made of other items. Copyright restrictions, about which library staff will advise, must be borne in mind, however. Moreover, some items may not copy well, or, as in the case of large-scale Ordnance Survey maps, may only be copiable on an A3 or larger sheet. For certain types of source, including local newspapers, indexes may have been compiled.

Local Records Offices
Written material is also available in local records offices, mostly in manuscript form. Some of it can be adapted to use with young children, school log-book entries providing one example. Records offices also keep printed material, including maps, newspapers and posters.

Local Museums
Local museums will usually be of particular help as far as artefacts are concerned. Sometimes, they have loan collections available and may offer replica artefacts for sale. They may also keep other types of source material, including photographs and posters. Again, copies of some of these items may be available for purchase. Many museums have an education officer, whose work involves school visits.

Other Local Organisations
Help in obtaining local history sources can be provided by several other local organisations. They include local history and photographic societies, art galleries, heritage centres, local newspapers, and film and sound archives. However, the type of source material they can offer, and their ability to help, will vary appreciably.

National Organisations
National organisations, including major museums, may also have material relating to particular localities. In the case of church schools, the National Society can be approached to obtain historical information on particular schools, including school plans. Its address is: National Society, Great Smith Street, London SW1P 3NP

A School Local History Collection
This can be built up gradually from:
• Copies of source material that various local organisations can offer.
• Material that individuals can supply. Oral testimony is the most obvious example but people will also provide personal archive material, of which, with permission, copies can be made. Such items as school reports, certificates of achievement, family photographs and letters fall into this category. Newspapers can prove highly effective.
• Contributions made by the children. Thus, the oral evidence they use may be entirely or largely self-generated. This has particular advantage in that the children will be helping to create an historical record.

The amount of source material in a school's local history collection need not be large. A limited, but well-chosen and varied selection is likely to prove highly effective in meeting Attainment Targets and Levels.

> **Finding local history sources**
>
> *Step 1* Make an appointment to see the staff at your local reference library, museum and/or records office.
> *Step 2* Explain fully what you want to do and seek advice as to what is feasible given the source material they can provide.
> *Step 3* Go through any catalogues or indexes they have.
> *Step 4* As you go through material, keep a note of the items you think might be useful, jotting down any reference numbers.
> *Step 5* Select material carefully, going for quality rather than quantity.

118 Schools 100 Years Ago

Background Information

In considering schooling around a century ago, the children will be examining an issue which was of great concern to contemporaries and which had an appreciable impact at local level. It was during this period that a major elementary school building programme took place, strongly inspired by the belief that Britain's relative economic decline was closely linked with deficiencies in education.

The school building programme was facilitated by several Acts of Parliament. Amongst them was Forster's 1870 Education Act. This aimed to establish new schools in districts where the voluntary system (churches and charities) was not making adequate provision. Local school boards were created in such districts, empowered to build and maintain schools. They were able to draw on rate aid, in addition to government grants and fees paid by the scholars. (Fees in elementary schools were not entirely abolished until 1918.) Sandon's Act of 1876 required that children aged ten to 14 must attend school half time (the half-time system lasted until 1918.) Mundella's Act of 1889 made full-time education obligatory for all children between the ages of five and ten.

The extent of school building in particular localities can be judged from the lists of school archives held in local records offices. For example, Bolton Archive Service preserves records of 106 local schools. In 70 cases, the records start between 1870 and 1910.

The School Premises

Classroom photographs taken in local schools are often available for the early 20th century and the children might compare them with the example shown. It should be remembered that classroom photographs were specially taken, so that wall displays and the appearance of teachers and pupils may have been rather different from normal.

Supplementary evidence on the design and appearance of early school buildings can be derived from surviving examples and from copies of architects' plans. Log-book extracts and oral testimony can also give useful information on such

AT 1: Knowledge and understanding of history

Level 2
(b) Consider why classrooms were fitted with high windows.
(c) Discuss how classrooms in a modern school differ from those in the past.

Level 3
(a) Describe how classrooms have changed since the early 20th century.
(b) Consider why classroom design has changed over this period.
(c) With the aid of a 1950s classroom photograph, describe differences between classrooms then and 50 years earlier.

Level 4
(a) Be aware that classrooms built long ago are still used, but that new ones have been built.
(b) Recognise that new schools have been built to replace old ones and to serve new housing areas.
(c) Describe different features of local schools around a century ago.

AT 2: Interpretations of history

Level 2
Find differences in two adults' accounts of what classrooms were like when they were children past.

Level 3
Test children's ability to distinguish between such statements of fact as 'Classrooms had an open fire' and such points of view as 'Classrooms were grim places to

Level 4
Consider how a single photograph might give a false impression of what classrooms were like a century ago.

AT 3: The use of historical sources

Level 2
Show how the plan of an early school can help to answer the question: 'What were school buildings like around a century ago?'

Level 3
Infer from a photograph that school classrooms a century ago were less comfortable and cheerful than classrooms today.

Level 4
Find out about the equipment used in local classrooms around a century ago, using photographs and log-book extracts.

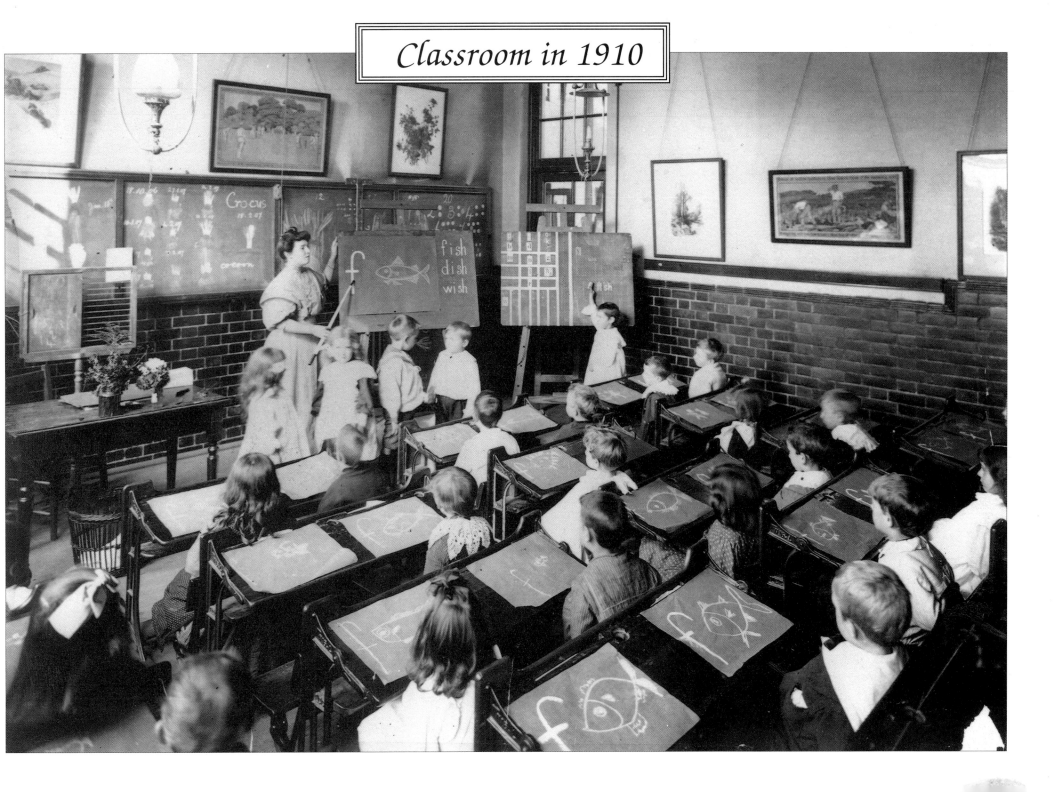

120 THE SCHOOL CURRICULUM

BACKGROUND INFORMATION

The Revised Code of 1862 introduced a payments-by-results system, government grants being given to schools on the basis of pupil attendance and the results of annual examinations in the three Rs. Other subjects, including geography, history, grammar and singing, also qualified for grant from the late 1860s, though limits were placed on the number that could be taken. Hence the school syllabus tended to focus on the three Rs.

In 1900, a block grant was introduced in place of payments by results, and this was accompanied by a list of subjects which would normally be taught. It comprised English, arithmetic, geography, history, singing, physical exercises, drawing for boys, and needlework for girls. Other subjects, such as science, were taught where practicable.

Abolishing payments by results helped to broaden the curriculum, and examples of subjects taught thereafter are commonly found in log-book entries. One of the most interesting is gardening, which was boosted by food shortages during World War 1. Impressive results could be obtained, as details in the log-book of Edgeside School show . They record the crop yields for 1918.

Oct 24th The following is a statement of the crops raised on the garden plot.

Potatoes	= 514 lbs
Cabbages	= 156 plants
Cauliflowers	= 30 "
Turnips	= 30 lbs
Lettuces	= 20 plants
Brussel Sprouts	= 36 "

Owing to the peas being set too late, they did not mature.

SCHOOL REPORTS

The children could use a copy of the report to consider the types of lesson children had around a century ago. Drawing especially on log-book evidence and oral testimony, they could explore how typical this was, noting any differences between subjects taught to boys and to girls. Comparisons with their own curriculum can be made, bringing out views about favourite and least favourite lessons.

AT1: Knowledge and understanding of history

Level 2
(b) Appreciate why, under the payment-by-results system, teachers were keen to teach the three Rs well.
(c) Note differences between their own curriculum and that of local schools in the past.

Level 3
(a) Describe changes that have occurred in the way children write.
(b) Appreciate that the school curriculum has changed because subjects such as science and technology have become more

Level 4
(a) Show an awareness that some subjects have long been taught in local schools whilst others are more recently introduced.
(b) Appreciate that the school curriculum has changed because some subjects have become more important and because of legal requirements.

AT 2: Interpretations of history

Level 3
Recognise that statements such as 'We had arithmetic lessons' are factual but those such as 'No one liked arithmetic lessons' are points of view.

Level 4
Appreciate that insufficient evidence may lead to differing interpretations about the range of school subjects taught in the past.

Report of Scholars Work

Term ended *Easter 1915*

Attendance Possible _*109*_ _
  Times absent _*30*_ _ _
  Times late _ *0* _ _ _

Name _ *Annie Almond* _
Position on Class List _ *7* _ _ _

Examination Results

Subject	Result
Arithmetic	g.
Reading	v. g.
Recitation	g.
Composition and Spelling	v. g.
Handwriting	g.
History	f. g.
Geography	f. g.
Hygiene	g.
Needlework	Ex.
Brush Drawing	f. g.
Music	f.

Remarks _*Annie is a steady*_ _ _ _
*industrious girl* _ _ _ _ _

Class Teacher _*E. Shaw*_ _
Head Teacher _*A Porter*_ _ _

AT 3: Use of historical sources

Level 2
Be aware that old classroom photographs can help to show what subjects were studied.

Level 3
Deduce from classroom photographs that children learned to write by copying sentences from the board.

Level 4
Assemble evidence from log-book extracts and oral testimony to determine the curriculum of local schools in the past.

School Report

Report of Scholars Work

Term ended Easter 1915

Attendance Possible _109_
Times absent _30_
Times late _0_

Name _ Annie Almond _
Position on Class List _ 7 _

Examination Results

Subject	Result
Arithmetic	G.
Reading	V. G.
Recitation	G.
Composition and Spelling	V. G.
Handwriting	G.
History	F. G.
Geography	F. G.
Hygiene	G.
Needlework	Ex.
Brush Drawing	F. G
Music	F.

Remarks _ Annie is a _ steady _
_ industrious _ girl _

Class Teacher _ E. Snee. _
Head Teacher _ A. Porter _

122 IN THE PLAYGROUND

BACKGROUND INFORMATION

During the late 19th century, much importance was attached to children's physical development. Drill, which comprised marching in different military formations, became widely practised. Log-book evidence suggests that it was mainly boys who were involved, though drill schemes were formulated for girls. Former soldiers might be employed to take drill lessons, which could last for an hour. The purpose behind drilling has been described by one historian as inculcating 'a sense of discipline and prompt obedience to orders amongst a large group of children'.

Some idea of the nature of drill can be obtained from the following details, extracted from a scheme prepared for Standard VI boys by the Birmingham School Board.
1. March at a uniform rate, at even distance, and with good carriage.
2. Change step, and do the right about turn on the march.
3. Counter-marching.
4. March in line backwards and forwards.
5. First simple figure march.
6. Marching in fours.

Other types of physical activity included Indian club and dumb-bell exercises, swimming and dancing.

With regard to playground games, oral testimony is unsurpassed. The popularity of certain games, the time of year they were played, and comparisons with present-day playground games are key themes to address.

PHOTOGRAPHS

Old photographs of pupils taking physical exercise in the school yard provide useful opportunities for teaching the children to ask questions of historical sources. These questions can focus on such matters as what the scholars in the picture are doing, where they are, what clothes they are wearing for the activity, whether these clothes are suitable, whether the children would have enjoyed the activity, and so on. By addressing such questions, the children will gain practice in looking carefully at an historical source rather than scanning it superficially. Comparisons with their own PE lessons can be usefully made.

AT 1: Knowledge and understanding of history

Level 2
(b) Suggest reasons why infants in the past had separate playgrounds from older children.
(c) Understand that pupils in the past had a long lunch break because they went home to eat.

Level 3
(a) Describe changes in the type of playground games children play now and in the past.
(b) Understand that pupils nowadays have shorter lunch breaks than in the past because school lunches are now available.

Level 4
(a) Identify changes in playground games since the early part of this century, as well as playground games that have remained popular.
(b) Recognise that school lunches were introduced because many parents welcomed them and because local education authorities felt they would improve children's health.

AT 3: The use of historical sources

Level 2
Recognise that photographs of playground activities in the past can stimulate questions about the type of outdoor lessons that pupils had in the past.

Level 3
Deduce from oral testimony that some playground games were more popular than others.

Level 4
Put together information from oral testimony and autobiographies to find out about the types of lunch local children were given in times past.

AT 2: Interpretations of history

Level 3
Recognise that a statement such as 'We played marbles in the playground' is fact, whereas a statement such as 'We didn't like playtimes on cold days' is a point of view.

Level 4
Understand that too little evidence may lead to differing interpretations about which were the most popular playground games amongst local pupils around a century ago.

In the Playground

124 TEACHING AND TEACHERS

BACKGROUND INFORMATION

This theme provides opportunities for the children to explore such issues as teaching methods, class size, the styles and the strictness of teachers. Oral and log-book evidence are especially valuable and can be used to draw contrasts with present-day teaching. However, these may not be as sharp as might appear. Thus, with regard to strictness, past pupils often remember that teachers made allowances for the circumstances in which children found themselves, and some teachers are remembered with affection. Again, acts of compassion on the part of teachers can be found amongst log-book entries, including visiting sick and dying children.

Useful insights into teaching methods can be gained from contemporaneous instruction manuals. That published by the Home and Colonial School Society in 1884, *A Course of Lessons for Infants*, is an excellent example. It spells out the teaching of numerous lessons in great detail, one of which could be chosen to recreate a lesson from the past. For instance, a lesson on the baker begins in the following way:

His work. Show some bread to the children and ask who made it. The baker. Repeat: 'The man who makes bread is called a baker.' Show a picture of a baker at work. Notice his dress. What colour is it? White. Why do the children think this colour is chosen?

The lesson proceeds with the teacher mixing dough, assisted by the children coming out to add ingredients.

LOG-BOOKS

Selected log-book entries can be used to give an impression of the way local teachers in the past treated their pupils. Extracts showing different attitudes can usually be found, not all suggesting harsh treatment. This type of evidence can then be compared with that derived from oral testimony, in order to build up a fuller, if still varied, picture.

AT 3: The use of historical sources

Level 2
Be aware that log-book entries can tell us something about the way local children were taught in the past, as well as raising questions about this issue, which can be tackled through oral history.

Level 3
Infer from old classroom photographs that teachers in the past were strict.

Level 4
Use oral evidence and log-book extracts to assess the attitudes local teachers in the past had towards their pupils.

AT 2: Interpretations of history

Level 2
Using oral testimony, recognise that former pupils can have differing impressions about how strict teachers were in the past.

Level 3
Understand that statements such as 'Teachers taught large classes' are factual, whereas those such as 'Nobody liked the headteacher' are points of view.

Level 4
Appreciate that lack of evidence may lead to different interpretations about the attitude teachers had to their pupils in the past.were used.

AT 1: Knowledge and understanding of history

Level 2
(b) Appreciate that teachers a century or so ago taught on a class basis because of large class sizes.
(c) Consider differences between today's teachers and teachers in the past.

Level 3
Describe changes that have occurred in the way children are taught.
(b) Be aware that teaching methods have changed because new technology (such as television and computers) have become available.
(c) Using classroom photographs from the early 1900s, the 1950s and today, consider differences in the way children are taught.

Level 4
(a) Appreciate that teachers today may use more group teaching than in the past, but that they often still teach on a class basis.
(b) Understand that teaching methods have changed because of new technology and because beliefs change about what is the best way to teach.

Log book extracts

April 4th	School opened this morning. New educational year commences today.
April 11th	Attendance Officer visited the school this morning.
April 15th	Owing to the severe cold of the school, all the children were taken for a Nature Ramble, commencing 2.30, at the suggestion of the Corresponding Manager.
April 22nd	On account of the uncertainty of the weather, the Time Table will not be strictly adhered to, until all the seeds are sown in the School Garden.
April 29th	Monthly Returns sent to Mr Bygrave.
May 3rd	The Religious Examination was held yesterday.
May 4th	The school will be closed tomorrow for the Feast of the Ascension.

126 SCHOLARS

BACKGROUND INFORMATION

Around the turn of the century, it was not uncommon for children to begin school before they reached five years of age. They would usually start in the 'babies' class and then progress through two infant classes before transferring to the junior school at the age of seven.

The Revised Code of 1862 stipulated that children were to be grouped into six standards according to their academic attainment. To cater for the growing number of pupils who were staying on longer at school, a new Standard VII was introduced in 1882. This system meant that children could remain in the lower standards if they failed to pass their annual examinations, resulting in classes with a wide age range. In fact, it is unlikely that many of them attained Standard VI or VII, as log-book entries suggest.

Although under Sandon's Act of 1876, children aged ten to fourteen were required to attend school half time, they could be exempt if they passed Standard IV and had made sufficient attendances. From 1880, however, exemption could be gained on attendance alone, giving rise to the so-called 'dunce's pass'. This exemption was controlled somewhat when the school-leaving age was raised for all pupils to 11 in 1893 and 12 in 1899. By the turn of the century, therefore, a child would need to have been 12 to go half-time and to have achieved a satisfactory attendance (sometimes referred to as 'getting enough days in') and/or passed Standard IV to leave altogether.

AT 1: Knowledge and understanding of history

Level 2
(a) Place writing instruments used by pupils (dip pen, fountain pen and felt tip) in chronological order.
(b) Suggest that the reasons for local children being absent from school included illness, helping with the harvest, and looking after younger brothers and sisters.
(c) Identify differences between the type of clothes local pupils wore in the past and the type they wear today.

Level 3
(a) Describe how the appearance of local pupils has changed over the last century.
(b) Understand that school attendance officers were appointed because many pupils were thought to be absent from school without good reason

Level 4
(a) Recognise that some local pupils' forenames have remained popular, whilst others have become less popular.
(b) Be aware that rises in the age at which children leave school has led to the building of many secondary schools and to many more pupils being educated to a higher standard.
(c) Describe the main features of local school life in the early 20th century.

AT 2: Interpretations of history

Level 3
Recognise that a statement such as 'I left school at 13' is factual, whilst one such as 'I would have done better if I had stayed longer at school' is a point of view.

Level 4
Appreciate that insufficient evidence may lead to differing interpretations about how frequently local pupils became part timers.

AT 3: The use of historical sources

Level 2
Recognise that log-book entries can shed a good deal of light on the question of how pupils were encouraged to attend local schools in the past.

Level 3
Deduce from oral testimony that pupils in the past were generally well behaved.

Level 4
Draw on log-book evidence, photographs and oral testimony to work out a typical day at school for children in the past.

20 — ST. JAMES'S ADMISSIONS REGISTER

NUMBER		DATE			NAME		BIRTH			PARENT OR GUARDIAN		FORMER SCHOOL	WITHDRAWAL			
Admission	Re-admission	Day	Month	Year			Day	Month	Year	Name	Address		Day	Month	Year	Cause
Evacuees 3831		14	8	44	Fiveash	Raymond	30	1	34	Mr. Hird.	25, Eldon Rd	Christ Church Forest Hill	29	1.	45	St. Barnabas
3832		"	"		Fiveash	Lauretta	18	8	36	R. Wilkinson	14, Eldon Rd	" "	29	1	45	London.
3833		"	"		Wilson	Thomas	3	4	34	Miss Ainsworth	86, Langham Rd.	Holbeach Rd Catford. S.E.6	5	2	45	"
3834		"	"		Wilson	John	2	11	36	Miss Bond.	7. Colenso Rd.	"	22	1	45	"
3835		"	"		Wilson	Doreen	26	7	35	Mrs. Priest.	29, Langham Rd.	"	25	6	45	"
3836		"	"		Roberts	Kenneth	29	8	35	Mr. Green.	107 Langham Rd	Brockley Rd. S.E.4	15	12	44	Halifax
3837		"	"		Roberts	Irene.	29	5	37	Mrs. Bolton	119, Langham Rd	"	15	12	44.	"
3838		"	"		Lambson	Albert Charles	6	12	34	R. Haworth.	42, Colenso Rd.	Turnham Rd. Brockley.	15	12	44.	London.
3839		"	"		Jeffries	Melinda Florence	28	4	36	H. Hinchley	112, Langham Rd.	Haseltine Rd. C.	11	5	45	London.
3840		"	"		Jeffries	Terence D.	8	5	36	R. Haworth.	104, Langham Rd.	Lower Sydenham. S.E.26	11	5	45	London.
3841	0	"	"		Bond	Mabel Susan	15	1	36	H. Wilkinson.	19, East Park Ave.	Christ Church.	19	1	45	Four Lanes End
3842		"	"		Bond	Rose Helena.	29	1	58	C. F. Sague.	23, East Park Ave.	Forest Hill. S.E.23	16	4	45	London.

ATTENDANCE REGISTERS

School-attendance registers provide useful insights into the ages at which children started and left school, the reasons for leaving, and the standard they attained. Such data can be fed into computer database programs, along with pupils' names and gender. Searches the children can undertake include forename popularity, commonest age of starting and leaving school and whether one gender tended to attain a higher level.

Attendance Register

ST. JAMES'S ADMISSIONS REGISTER

20

NUMBER		DATE			NAME	BIRTH			PARENT OR GUARDIAN		FORMER SCHOOL	WITHDRAWAL			
Admission	Re-admission	Day	Month	Year		Day	Month	Year	Name	Address		Day	Month	Year	Cause
Evacuees															
3831		14	8	44	Fiveash Raymond	30	1	34	Mr. Hird	25, Eldon Rd	Christ Church Forest Hill	29	1	45	St. Barnabas
3832		"			Fiveash Lauretta	18	8	36	R. Wilkinson	14, Eldon Rd	" "	29	1	45	"
3833		"			Wilson Thomas	3	4	34	Miss Ainsworth	86, Langham Rd	Holbeach Rd Catford S.E.6	5	2	45	London
3834		"			Wilson John	2	11	36	Miss Bond	7. Colenso Rd	"	22	1	45	"
3835		"			Wilson Doreen	26	7	35	Mrs. Prest	29, Langham Rd	"	23	6	45	"
3836		"			Roberts Kenneth	29	8	35	Mrs. Green	107 Langham Rd	Brockley Rd. S.E.4	15	12	44	Halifax
3837		"			Roberts Irene	29	5	37	Mrs. Bolton	119, Langham Rd	"	15	12	44	"
3838		"			Lambson Albert Charles	6	12	33	R. Haworth	42, Colenso Rd	Turnham Rd Brockley	15	12	44	London
3839		"			Jeffries Melinda Florence	28	4	35	H. Hinchley	112, Langham Rd	Haseltine Rd. C.	11	5	45	London
3840		"			Jeffries Terence D.	8	5	36	R. Haworth	104, Langham Rd	Lower Sydenham S.E.26	11	5	45	London
3841	0	"			Bond Mabel Susan	15	1	36	H. Wilkinson	19, East Park Ave	Christ Church	19	1	45	Four Lanes End
3842		"			Bond Rose Helena	29	1	38	C.F. Sager	23, East Park Ave.	Forest Hill S.E.23	16	4	45	London
3843		"			Mills Grace Edith	23	2	35	M. Holden	131, Langham Rd	Torridon Rd.	22	6	45	London
3844		"			Mills Brian	30	1	39	H. Walmsley	97, St James' Rd	Catford S.E.6	22	6	45	London
3845		"			Miles Kathleen	4	2	35	H Egan	21, Eldon Rd	Haseltine Rd.	29	9	44	London
3846		"			Miles Patricia	19	4	36			Lower Sydenham S.E.26	29	9	44	
3847		"			Delaney Kathleen	9	4	36	R. Walmsley	6, Linden Ave	Turnham Rd.	22	6	45	London
3848		"			Delaney Maureen	9	3	39	"		Brockley S.E.4	13	11	44	London
3849		"			Kimber James	10	12	39	Mrs. Bolton	72, Langham Rd.	Ennersdale Rd Lewisham	20	10	44	London
3850		"			Chadwick Alan E.	7	11	38	Mrs. Chadwick % 16, Winston Rd		Hugh Middleton Sch. EC	1.15	9	44	London
3851		"			Pollard Margaret Anne	11	12	36	G. Leach	127, Langham Rd	St. Paul's Mill Hill N.W.7	15	9	44	London
3852		"			Austen Roy Victor	16	9	36		31, Eldon Rd	Torridon Rd. Catford S.E.6 Forest Hill S.E	1	4	45	London
3853		"			Craddock Ronald	6	8	36	Mrs. Craddock % 72, Holly St.		Rathfern Rd.	29	9	44	London
3854		"			Coasby James	13	3	37	E. Stevenson	9, Beresford Rd	Downderry School Downham Bromley Kent	29	9	44	London
3855		"			Mummery Doris	4	5	38	Mrs. Bell	118, London Rd		11	12	44	London
3856		"			Monkhouse Patricia	21	4	37	G Sutcliffe	St. James' Rd		22	9	44	Keighley
3857		"			Monkhouse David	8	3	40	"	"		22	9	44	"
3858		"			Grimes Alan Kenneth	26	6	34	Mrs. Grimes % 13, St James' Rd		Devon Council Bexhill	29	9	44	London

SCHOOL PREMISES

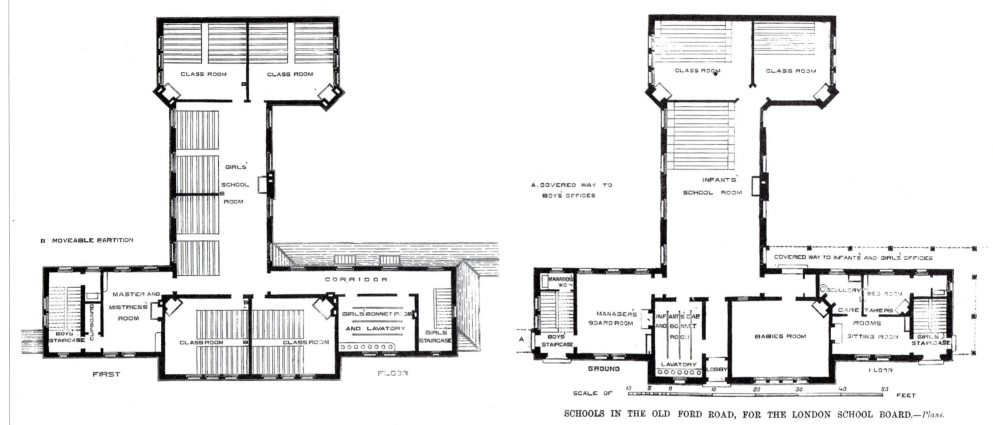

SCHOOLS IN THE OLD FORD ROAD, FOR THE LONDON SCHOOL BOARD.—*Plans.*

Using School Plans
Try to obtain plans of your own school and of local schools 100 years ago, from school archives, governors, education offices, local records office, diocesan authorities etc.

The plan shown here is not untypical of schools built in the 1890s and can be used for comparative work.

Simple Map Interpretation
How many classrooms?
What were the areas designed for?
Where are the toilets on the plan?
How many toilets?
Compare words used then and now.

Combining Sources
This and other plans can be used alongside other resource pages from this book such as the classroom photograph on page 119.

Enlarge the plan. Ask the children to draw on the furniture arrangement they think might have existed in the school. They should use the photograph to make deductions.

Compare the front elevation and windows with those shown in the photograph.

Could the classroom in the photograph be a classroom on the plan? Ask the children to give reasons for their answers.

Using the drill lesson on page 123, ask the children to identify places on the plan where drill might have taken place. Compare the exterior of the school with the elevation shown here.

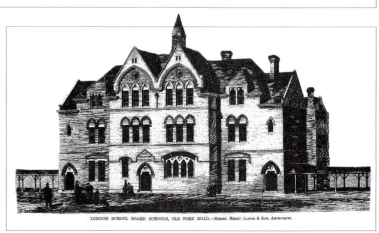

LONDON SCHOOL BOARD SCHOOLS, OLD FORD ROAD.—Messrs. Henry Jarvis & Son, Architects.